JUST
CHICKEN

THOMAS HINDE &
CORDELIA CHITTY

JUST CHICKEN

MENU
FEATHER FOWLIE
CHICKEN MARENGO
JUTLAND BLUE

BANTAM PRESS

NEW YORK · LONDON · TORONTO · SYDNEY · AUCKLAND

Cartoonist: William Belcher

We would like to thank the British Chicken Information Service for their help and support.

Transworld Publishers Ltd.,
Century House,
61-63 Uxbridge Road,
London W5 5SA.

Transworld Publishers (Australia) Pty Ltd.,
26 Harley Crescent,
Condell Park,
NSW 2200.

Transworld Publishers (NZ) Ltd.,
Cnr. Moselle & Waipareira Aves,
Henderson,
Auckland.

Published 1986 by Bantam Press, a division of Transworld Publishers Ltd.

A PHOEBE PHILLIPS EDITIONS BOOK

Design and illustrations copyright © Phoebe Phillips Editions 1985.
Text copyright © Thomas Hinde and Cordelia Chitty 1985

British Library Cataloguing in Publication Data
Hinde, Thomas
　Just chicken.
　1. Cookery (Chicken)
　Rn: Sir Thomas Willes Chitty　　I. Title
　II. Chitty, Cordelia
　641.6'65　TX750

ISBN 0-593-01028-0

Printed and bound in Great Britain

CONTENTS

INTRODUCTION

'Chicken makes the meal,' the Spanish say. Long before I heard this I thought of chicken as something special. It arrived for lunch on occasional Sundays, in place of the usual fatty leg of mutton, or sinewy sirloin of beef. And it was cooked in just two ways: roast or boiled. I continue to think fondly of those great pre-war birds – six-pounders, at least, in my imagination – crisply brown with Brussels sprouts and roast potatoes, or creamy and tender, with egg sauce, and the fact that their present-day smaller relations have become the most economical food you can buy still seems something of a miracle.

During the War my family continued to be closely connected with chickens. Our cockerels, hatched by the mother of the flock, a huge Rhode Island Red named Beauty, of course went into the pot. But so did any hen rash enough to have a prolonged moult, or which began to 'mope'. Our aim was to forestall the later stages of a complaint which we unscientifically called 'going light'. I well remember my mother discovering how to turn such aged boilers into roasters by first simmering them for a couple of hours then roasting them for an hour in a hot oven. One other dish she developed in those days of food rationing was Chicken Rice (see page 120), to make use of leftovers.

So it wasn't till my wife and I began to cook for ourselves in a more adventurous way, and later when our daughter, Cordelia, emerged from the cake-and-sticky-bun period to join us, that we discovered the many other possibilities of chicken. The Spanish are right. Quite simply, it is by far the most adaptable of all meats.

The reasons are not hard to discover: the tenderness of the flesh of a young chicken – or even an old one when properly treated; the way in which this varies on any one bird, so that different joints have different characteristics and suit different dishes; above all, the fact that chicken meat does *not* itself have too strong a flavour, and as a result can be blended with such a wide variety of other flavours.

As if this were not enough, a chicken comes with a deliciously tender and flavourful liver, an excellent basis for a wide range of pâtés and terrines, and the stock you can make from its bones not only forms the basis of many of the best soups but is an important ingredient of a number of other dishes.

This book gathers together the discoveries which Cordelia and I have made. They range from simple stews to complicated creations like Grilled Chicken Maintenon (see page 92), developed by Louis XIV's chef in honour of the king's mistress. In selecting them we worked on two principles. The first was that they should be as varied as possible. Even now, we continue to be astonished at the way in which a new recipe can transform a basic frozen roaster into a totally new culinary experience. We include dishes from twenty-four countries.

The second was that each in its own way should be delicious. As a result, you will find a fair proportion of classic chicken dishes, from Coq au Vin (see page 102) to Paella (see page 89). But for these two in particular, as well as for many others, it took much research to discover a recipe which really works. Every one of them we have tested, most of them many times, and we try to explain our methods clearly and simply.

Neither of us has ever taken a cookery lesson (except from each other) and it is our belief that almost everyone can turn himself or herself into a competent cook provided they can read a recipe book and they relish the results. If this is true of cooking in general, it is particularly so of chicken cooking. One or two of our recipes take time, trouble and care, but none are really difficult in the way that the elaborate creations of pastry cooking could be said to be.

We have divided the main-course recipes according to their ease or complication rather than the time they take. One or two of the very simple ones need long, slow cooking. In the other sections you will find some dishes which could equally well be eaten as hot main courses – the two pies, for example – but we have separated them when, in our opinion, they are better cold, and because it may be convenient to find possible picnic dishes collected in one place.

The quantities we give for most of the recipes make a dish for six people. By using a larger bird and increasing the other ingredients proportionately, you can almost always expand them to make sufficient for eight, perhaps even ten people. For more than this we suggest using a second bird.

We have given both imperial and metric measurements, but do not mix them within a recipe. Spoon measurements for dry ingredients are very slightly rounded unless otherwise stated.

Whenever the oven is used it should be preheated. We have given the temperatures with the ingredients so that you will be able to see at a glance for which recipes you will need the oven. Occasionally it is not needed until well towards the end of the cooking time.

Occasionally, dishes require cooking at very low temperatures. Our oven functions well at the temperatures given in these recipes, but do check the lowest temperature at which yours is efficient and use that. Also, test that the meat is cooked – just stick a skewer into it and make sure the juices are clear.

FOOD VALUE

As well as being the most adaptable of meats, chicken is the healthiest. It is low in calories, containing less fat than beef, veal, mutton, lamb or even turkey. The breast is the least fatty and the skin most fatty. A few of our recipes specifically require the skin, but for many others, even when we don't say so, the skin could be removed and discarded.

On the other hand, chicken is rich in protein and also contains some of the B group of vitamins, and useful minerals. For all these reasons it is much favoured by those who need to lose weight but enjoy good food.

If you are concerned about calories substitute a low-fat spread for the butter or oil we have specified for frying or for roasting or when making roux-based sauces. If concerned about cholesterol, use a polyunsaturated fat or oil.

Types of chicken

Poussin

A poussin is a very young chicken about 4-6 weeks of age and weighing from 1-2 pounds (450 g-1 kg). One bird will give one or two portions, depending on the size. Poussins should be fried, roasted or grilled. Young chickens of 10-12 weeks are also available. They weigh 2-3 pounds (1-1.5 kg) and give 3-4 portions. They can be roasted, fried or grilled.

Roasting chicken or broiler

Roasting chicken, or broilers, are the most popular type of chicken. They generally weigh between 2½-4 pounds (1.25-1.75 kg), but may be up to 7 pounds (3 kg), are aged between 5 months and a year and will give 6-8 portions. This type of chicken can be casseroled, roasted, grilled or fried. Most chicken joints that are sold come from this type of bird.

Boiler or stewing fowl

A boiler or stewing fowl is an older bird weighing 4-7 pounds (1.75-3 kg) and giving 6-10 portions. It tends to be less popular nowadays, perhaps because its flesh is tougher and it will have more fat. However, the ample meat has more flavour than that of a roaster and is extremely good if cooked by a slow, moist method such as poaching or casseroling.

Maize-fed or corn-fed chicken

Maize or corn-fed chicken are becoming increasingly popular although they are more expensive than normal birds. The maize, or sweetcorn, on which the birds feed produces flesh that is yellow and well flavoured. It is suitable for all types of cooking, but it is best used for dishes that are not strongly flavoured so that the taste of the chicken will stand out.

Choosing and buying

Frozen chickens

When buying these take the sort of sensible precautions you would take when buying any frozen food. See that the bird's proper sale date (if given) has not passed, that the wrapping has not been damaged and that there are no discoloured patches.

Fresh chickens

Most chickens sold as 'fresh' have been reared by the same intensive methods as frozen chickens, but they should have a better flavour. Occasional quality butchers may sell genuine 'farmyard' or free-range birds. Your best guide to quality is the reliability of the shop or butcher you are buying from.

From the farm

Chickens bought from a farm may also be either

free-range or intensively reared. Also, some egg-producing farms sell their laying birds when they have finished their first season, and these can be a bargain. They should be treated as old birds, and will have the good flavour of a boiling fowl. However, you will probably have to pluck, draw and perhaps even kill them yourself. To improve their quality follow the old country practice of killing, plucking and removing their intestines and crops, but leaving on their heads and feet and hanging them for 2 or 3 days.

Joints
Chicken joints are available fresh or frozen. They are convenient for dishes requiring a particular cut, but they are seldom good value. It is better to buy a whole bird and use the parts not wanted in one recipe in another dish.

Livers
Twenty years ago in some areas these were lumped together with necks, hearts and gizzards and sold cheaply for cat food. Alas, they are now expensive. A single liver from one bird may not be of use on its own so keep a packet of livers in the freezer and keep adding to it until you have enough to make a pâté.

Preparation

PLUCKING
Plucking is not difficult, although it is tedious, particularly if the bird was moulting when it was killed and covered with feathers that have only partly emerged. Chickens are easiest to pluck immediately after they have been killed, but we leave them until they are cold because the skin is then less easily torn. Simply pull away the body feathers in tufts, pulling in the opposite direction to

the way they naturally lie, then pull out the large wing and tail feathers one at a time, using pliers if necessary. Finally, singe the body fluff.

DRAWING
1. Cut the feet off just below the knees.
2. Cut the head off about 3 inches (7.5 cm) from the shoulders.
3. Open and push back the skin around the remaining 3 inches (7.5 cm) of neck and cut the neck off close to the shoulders, then remove the crop and windpipe.
4. With a sharp knife, cut round the vent, then cut the skin upwards as far as the rear end of the breast bone.
5. Insert your hand (wear a thin rubber glove if you feel a little squeamish) and pull out all the intestines together.
6. Separate and set aside the liver and heart, first cutting out and discarding the liver's small green gall bladder, taking care not to break it. Its bitter contents can ruin the taste of any part of a chicken that it contaminates.
7. Slice the gizzard in half, wash out its contents and remove the tough, wrinkled inner skin. The flesh of the gizzard is edible and can, for example, be minced and added to a stuffing, but it is usually best simmered with the neck and bones for stock.
8. Wipe the chicken inside and out with a damp cloth.

THAWING
The usual advice given is that a 3½-4 pound (1.5-1.75 kg) frozen chicken must be allowed at least 24 hours to thaw in a refrigerator or 8-9 hours at room temperature, longer if your kitchen is cold. In practice, you can hurry the process by standing the bird, still in its plastic wrapper, in cold water. Don't forget to remove the polythene bag of giblets and neck that are often put into the cavity of commercially frozen birds and *never* cook a bird

which has not completely thawed. There may be bacteria in the cavity which, if not destroyed during the cooking, can make you seriously ill.

If in doubt, just place your thumb in the cavity of the bird and forefinger on the outside and press. If it feels soft to the touch the bird is thawed – ice crystals would remain solid.

STUFFING AND TRUSSING

The purpose of trussing a chicken is to hold it in shape when it is cooked.

1. Turn the bird on to its breast and fold its wings behind its back.

2. Place some stuffing under the loose skin around the neck then bring the skin down the back and hold it in place with a skewer that also passes from one side of the bird to the other through both wings.

3. Turn the bird on its back, place some stuffing in the cavity and sew up the skin.

4. Press down the legs and pass a skewer through them, and through the body, at the point where the thighs and drumsticks meet.

5. Tie the legs close together with string by looping them just above the knees, and draw them downwards by taking a final loop around the parson's nose.

Nowadays nearly all pre-packaged birds, whether fresh or frozen, are sold ready trussed, and all that is necessary is to remove any giblets then stuff the cavity as described above.

JOINTING

A chicken divides conveniently into 10 joints, but the two parts of the back and the two wings will only make meagre servings on their own.

1. Cut off the outer sections of each wing at the final joint and the lower legs at the knee joints and use these for stock.

2. Set the chicken on its back, force one complete leg away from the body then cut it off, feeling with the knife to find the thigh joint.
3. Divide the drumstick from the thigh, again at the joint.
4. Repeat for the other leg.
5. Cut off the remaining two sections of each wing where they join the body.
6. Separate the breast from the back by cutting through the rib bones on each side.
7. Divide the back into two by cutting across it.
8. Cut the breast into two by first dividing it at the neck end, cutting through the wishbone, then cutting downwards alongside the breastbone.
9. To make more, but smaller, pieces, subdivide each breast, wing and thigh.

BONING A CHICKEN

Here are two methods of boning a chicken. Method B is a good deal more simple than A but it is less thorough, so for certain dishes you will need to use the more difficult first method. For both you must use a very sharp knife, but be careful not to pierce the skin – apart from the initial cut in B.

Method A
1. Working from the neck end, loosen the skin from the flesh around the neck opening and cut the wishbone out from within the flesh.
2. Locate the shoulder joints on each side of the neck and sever.
3. Cut the flesh away from the bones in the first section of the wings and remove the bones.
4. Carefully extract the two outer wing bones – the wing tips can be cut off.
5. Now start to work on the thighs. First loosen the skin and flesh so that you can cut through the top joint. Cut the flesh away from the thigh bones and

break or cut the middle joint. Remove the thigh bones.

6. Work down the lower leg bones (drumsticks) and remove them. Leave the final pieces of leg beyond the drumsticks.

7. Cut away the flesh and skin around the central carcass. This must be done slowly and carefully in order not to break the skin. Pull out the carcass when it is loose.

Method B

1. Turn the chicken on to its breast, cut down the centre line of the back, then work outwards and downwards, separating the flesh from the skeleton and taking out the thigh bones, wishbone and inner wing bones as you reach them.

2. Remove the whole central skeleton when it is loose.

CHICKEN FILLETS
The method described below will give 2-4 fillets from the breast and two from the drumsticks.

Breast fillets
Divide the breast in two, then separate the flesh from the breastbone and rib cage.

Scrape the meat gently away from the bones, making sure you do not tear it as you ease it off.

If they are large, each of the two fillets can be halved to give a total of four fillets from the breast.

Drumstick and thigh fillets
Snap the joint at the bottom of the drumstick (just bend it back on itself) and cut through the tendons. With a small sharp knife, make a lengthways slit down to the bone. Scrape the flesh away from the bone. Repeat with the other drumstick.

Use the same technique to remove the flesh from the thigh-bones.

Basic cooking methods

BOILING

This is really a misnomer as the water should only be just simmering, otherwise the flesh can become tough and dry. It is an ideal way of cooking a boiler or stewing fowl as it tenderises their otherwise tough flesh yet keeps it moist. Put the bird into a pan, just cover with cold water and add 1 onion, a bay leaf, a sprig of fresh thyme or rosemary, 6 black peppercorns and 2 teaspoons salt. Bring just to the boil, lower the heat, cover and simmer gently for 35-40 minutes per pound (75-85 minutes per kg). It is also a good way of cooking roasting chickens that are to be served cold. Reduce the cooking time to 25 minutes then allow the bird to cool in the water.

ROASTING

Put into a baking tin with hot fat, place in a preheated oven and baste regularly to keep the flesh moist and to get a crisp skin. Allow 15 minutes per pound (30 minutes per kg) plus 15 minutes (weight after stuffing) at 425°F (220°C) gas mark 7, or 20 minutes per pound (40 minutes per kg) plus 15 minutes at 375-400°F (190-200°C) gas mark 5-6. We give some variations to this procedure.

To roast a boiler, first simmer it gently (with the flavourings suggested above) for 2 hours. Allow it to cool before stuffing it, then roast for the time appropriate to a roaster of the same weight.

SPIT-ROASTING

This is a popular method of cooking poussins. They are often split down the back-bone and opened out flat. Cook for about 45 minutes at 400-425°F (200-220°C) gas mark 6-7, basting frequently.

GRILLING

Poussins, chicken halves or chicken joints can be grilled. Place the chicken 3-4 inches (7.5-10 cm) below a moderately hot grill and cook for 8-15 minutes on each side, depending on size, turning them twice and basting with butter or oil occasionally.

FRYING
This method is used for chicken joints. Put the joints into a generous amount of hot oil or butter and fry until crisp and brown on both sides, then lower the heat and cook for a further 20 minutes, turning once.

CASSEROLING
This is good for either a roasting chicken or a boiling fowl, but at least double the cooking time is needed for a boiler.

Fry the chicken first to seal it, then add vegetables and other ingredients and finally pour on the liquid. The casserole is then covered and either simmered gently on top of the stove for about 1¼ hours or cooked in an oven preheated to 350°F (180°C) gas mark 4 for 1 hour. For chicken joints the time can be reduced to about 40 minutes.

MICROWAVE OVENS
We have not given special instructions for a microwave oven, but if you are an experienced microwave user, or have a good microwave recipe book, it will be easy to adapt them.

A microwave oven can be a great help for rapidly thawing a frozen bird, or a cooked dish. As a rough guide, thaw a frozen bird for 6-7 minutes per pound (12-14 minutes per kg) on 'full' power, 5 minutes resting then 3-4 minutes per pound (6-8 minutes per kg) on 'low' and another 5 minutes resting, or 6-7 minutes per pound (12-14 minutes per kg) on 'medium' then 20-30 minutes resting. But do check with the instruction book.

Carving

Arm yourself with a sharp knife and a carving fork so that you can hold the bird steady.

1. Leave a freshly cooked bird covered in a warm place for 10-15 minutes before carving it.

2. Remove any trussing skewers or string.

3. Take the end of one drumstick in your fingers, use it to move the whole leg away from the body and cut through the joint between the thigh and the body.

4. Cut the thigh and the drumstick apart at their joint and, if large, carve them into slices.

5. Cut off the wing on the same side, taking with it some of the adjoining breast.

6. Cut off the wishbone and surrounding flesh.

7. Cut downward slices from this side of the breast.

8. Carve the other side in a similar way.

Preserving

FREEZING

To keep bought frozen chickens, simply put them in your own freezer. The recommended storage time for poussins, spring chickens and roasting chickens is three months. After this time a frozen chicken's bones may darken and there is said to be a slow deterioration in their flavour, but in our experience not a dramatic one and, in practice, they can be kept much longer.

To freeze fresh chickens, choose young, plump, good-quality birds. Pluck and draw them if necessary and truss them. Cover any protruding bones with foil then put birds, individually, into freezer-proof polythene bags, excluding as much air as possible and sealing the bags tightly. Or wrap each bird closely in freezer-proof polythene, again excluding as much air as possible. Freeze the giblets separately. Wrap joints in the same way. Keep implements, hands and the birds clean.

Many of our dishes can be frozen and we have marked the most suitable ones*. Some others, such as casseroles thickened at the end of the cooking with egg yolks, can be frozen before the yolks are added. These are marked* at the appropriate stage. Simply put the dish into a clean bowl, and the bowl into a freezer bag, cool overnight in the refrigerator then place in the freezer. The dishes will keep for 2-3 months, but after this they *do* lose flavour. To thaw a casserole, leave it in the refrigerator overnight then place in a covered dish and reheat thoroughly – about 30 minutes at 350°F (180°C) gas mark 4. Make sure there is sufficient liquid in the dish and stir it occasionally. If you froze the dish before completing the recipe, follow the instructions from then on.

OTHER METHODS

Nowadays, when all sorts of chickens can be bought all the year round and kept for months in the freezer, the traditional methods for preserving chicken have virtually disappeared. However, chicken can be salted in brine to give an interesting, different flavour to the flesh.

SALTING IN BRINE

To make the brine, boil 12 ounces (350 g) unrefined salt, 8 ounces (225 g) brown sugar, 1 ounce (25 g) saltpetre, 1 bay leaf, 1 sprig of fresh thyme, 5 black peppercorns and 5 juniper berries in 3½ pints (2 litres) water for 5 minutes. Strain the brine into a plastic bucket or stoneware bowl and leave to cool. Lower in the chicken and keep it entirely submerged, if necessary with a weighted plate.

Stand the bucket or bowl in a cool place, and leave the chicken there for at least 2 days, and up to 3 weeks. The longer the chicken is left in the brine the more salt it will absorb. After two days it will need rinsing under a cold tap. After 2 or 3 weeks it will need standing in cold water for an hour. Chickens preserved in brine can simply be roasted when their special quality will be most obvious, or they can be used for most of our casseroles for an interesting variation.

Acknowledgements

We would like to thank all who have helped us. Some we mention for their particular suggestions. Others include Felicity Bettinson, Sheila Glossop, Charles Hodgson, Karen Robinson, Christopher Sales and Elisabeth Whipp. Our families have taken a keen interest and given much helpful advice.

RICH CHICKEN STOCK*

A good chicken stock is the basis of many of our sauces and most of our soups. Just boiling chicken bones and perhaps the skin may be enough for some purposes, but the recipe we give below produces the sort of strong-flavoured stock that is essential for many dishes. Whenever possible, make stock beforehand so that it can be cooled and the fat removed from the surface. Keep the stock in the refrigerator, reboiling it every other day or so. It can also be frozen – a useful standby when you haven't time to make fresh stock.

bones and leftovers from a cooked chicken, or the raw carcass, giblets except the liver, and bones, of a boned chicken
1 large onion, quartered
1 carrot, cut in half
10 black peppercorns,

2 bay leaves
salt

Preparation 5 minutes
Cooking 1¼ hours
Cooling 1½-2 hours

1. Put all the ingredients into a large saucepan, add 4 pints (2.25 litres) water, bring to the boil and simmer, covered, for at least 45 minutes, skimming off any scum that rises to the surface.
2. Strain and cool.
3. Remove the fat from the surface.

CLEAR CONSOMMÉ

This is how to turn chicken stock (opposite) into chicken consommé.

4 pints (2.25 litres) chicken stock (opposite)
2 egg whites, whisked
2 egg shells, crushed

Preparation 5 minutes
Cooking 1 hour 35 minutes

MENU PLANNING: Serve with thin brown toast. Drink dry sherry.

1. Boil the stock until reduced by half.
2. Add the egg whites and shells to the stock and heat to a rapid boil.
3. Leave to cool for 10 minutes.
4. Strain through cheese-cloth or muslin.
5. Reheat and serve hot, or allow to cool and serve as a jelly.

COCK-A-LEEKIE*

This wonderfully rich old Scottish soup is really a main course. Some recipes suggest using a 2 lb (1 kg) piece of stewing beef as well as the chicken, but we usually make do with beef stock. If making the stock from cubes do not add any salt at the beginning and check the level before serving. The beef flavour goes excellently with the prunes.

4 lb (1.75 kg) boiling fowl
2 pints (1.2 litres) beef stock, made with 2 cubes if necessary
8 peppercorns
salt
8 leeks, cleaned

8 ounces (225 g) prunes, soaked for 6 hours and stoned
For the garnish
chopped fresh parsley

Preparation 10 minutes
Cooking 3 hours

MENU PLANNING: A main-course soup. Serve with a celery, beetroot and apple salad.

1. Cover the chicken with the stock, add the peppercorns and salt, if necessary. Bring to the boil and remove the scum from the surface.
2. Tie 2 of the leeks together and put into the boiling stock. Cover and simmer for 2½ hours.
3. Chop the remaining leeks into 1 inch (2.5 cm) lengths and add to the stock, along with the prunes, either cut into halves or left whole, and simmer for 15 minutes.
4. Discard the leek bundle and remove the chicken. Allow it to cool slightly before taking off the skin and removing the flesh from the bones.
5. Roughly chop the flesh and return it to the soup. Reheat and sprinkle with chopped parsley.

HEARTY LENTIL SOUP

Do not serve this splendidly sustaining soup to start a meal because it *is* a meal. It makes a good supper – after an indulgent lunch.

2 ounces (50 g) red lentils
2 ounces (50 g) rolled oats
2 pints (1.2 litres) chicken stock (see page 22)
2 medium onions, chopped
8 ounces (225 g) peeled potatoes, sliced
¼ pint (150 ml) thin cream
4 ounces (100 g) cooked chicken, diced

salt and black pepper
2 slices of streaky bacon, diced

Soaking 1 hour
Preparation 5 minutes
Cooking 1 hour 5 minutes

MENU PLANNING: Eat with wholemeal bread and follow with a salad and cheese.

1. In a large saucepan, soak the lentils and the oats in the chicken stock for 1 hour.
2. Bring to the boil then simmer, covered, for 30 minutes.
3. Add the onions and potatoes and simmer, covered, for 25 minutes.*
4. Stir in the cream and chicken and reheat but do not boil.
5. Taste for seasoning.
6. Meanwhile, fry the bacon until crisp and drain on absorbent paper.
7. Serve the soup with the bacon sprinkled on top.

CORN CHOWDER

For this variation on a traditional New England chowder, half the sweetcorn should be 'cream style', but if that is not available ordinary sweetcorn kernels will do.

4 slices of streaky bacon, diced
8 ounces (225 g) onions, chopped
butter for frying, if necessary
1¼ pints (750 ml) chicken stock (see page 22)
8 ounces (225 g) potatoes, diced
7 ounce (200 g) can of sweetcorn kernels, drained
7 ounce (200 g) can creamed sweetcorn

8 ounces (225 g) cooked chicken, diced
8 fluid ounces (225 ml) thin cream
salt and black pepper
For the garnish
chopped parsley

Preparation 15 minutes
Cooking 30 minutes

MENU PLANNING: Serve with toast.
Drink a dry white wine.

1. In a large heavy saucepan, fry the bacon in its own fat until crisp, then remove with a slotted spoon and drain on absorbent paper. Crumble.
2. Fry the onions in the bacon fat, plus a little butter if necessary, until soft.
3. Pour the stock into the pan with the onions, add the potatoes, and simmer, covered, until the potatoes are cooked – about 15 minutes.
4. Add the sweetcorn, chicken, cream, salt and pepper and reheat but don't boil.
5. Sprinkle each serving with crumbled bacon and garnish with chopped parsley.

CHICKEN CREAM

This is a good way to use the backs, wings and neck of a chicken. Alternatively you can use 2-3 ounces (50-75 g) cooked chicken, and stock that has been made separately. Left-over creamy meat from Chicken Vallé d'Auge (see page 78) is particularly suitable and the resulting soup is especially sustaining.

wings, back, neck and, if available, bones of one chicken
6 black peppercorns
2 bay leaves
8 fluid ounces (225 ml) thick cream
1 tablespoon plain yoghurt
2 egg yolks
4-6 ounces (100-175 g) boiled potatoes, diced

2-3 ounces (50-75 g) fried onions
salt and black pepper

Preparation 20 minutes
Cooking 2 hours

MENU PLANNING: A rich soup to precede a simple main course.

1. In a large, covered saucepan, simmer the wings, back, neck and bones with the peppercorns and bay leaves in 2 pints (1.2 litres) water.
2. Strain.
3. Remove the meat from the bones and chop it finely.
4. Gradually blend the cream and yoghurt into the egg yolks then whisk into 1½ pints (900 ml) of the stock.
5. Add the potatoes, onions and chicken and heat through gently, stirring constantly, but do not allow the soup to boil.
6. Taste for seasoning, and serve.

FEATHER FOWLIE*

An old Scottish soup. We use a little lemon juice to perk it up and serve the cream separately so that it can be added just before the soup is eaten. You really need a blender or liquidiser, but you can use a mincer if necessary.

4 lb (1.75 kg) boiling fowl
2 onions, roughly chopped
3 carrots, roughly chopped
1 turnip, roughly chopped
3 sticks of celery, roughly chopped
1 teaspoon dried mixed herbs
salt
12 black peppercorns
2 ounces (50 g) ground almonds

3 ounces (75 g) fresh white breadcrumbs
juice from ½-1 lemon
For the garnish
chopped fresh parsley
For serving
¼ pint (150 ml) thick cream

Preparation 15 minutes
Cooking 3½ hours

MENU PLANNING: Precede with a small glass of neat Scotch and follow with an egg dish.

1. Put the chicken, vegetables, mixed herbs, salt and peppercorns into a large saucepan, cover with cold water, bring to the boil and simmer, covered, for 2-2½ hours, removing any scum that forms.
2. Remove the chicken and allow to cool slightly before removing the skin and taking the meat from the bones.
3. Strain the vegetables, keeping the stock, and purée both the chicken and vegetables in a blender or food processor. Alternatively, mash the vegetables and mince the chicken.
4. Return the chicken and vegetable purée to a large pan and stir in the ground almonds and breadcrumbs.
5. Gradually stir about 2 pints (1.2 litres) of the stock into the chicken. Return to the heat and simmer, uncovered, for 30 minutes, stirring occasionally.
6. Add lemon juice to taste.
7. Garnish with parsley and serve the cream separately.

VELOUTÉ DE VOLAILLE

A soup that specifically requests giblets for the basic stock, although you would never guess it from the delicate result. It must be eaten as soon as made, although the stock can be prepared in advance.

giblets from 2 chickens
2 carrots, roughly chopped
2 leeks, roughly chopped
1 stick of celery, roughly
    chopped
1 onion, roughly chopped
1 clove of garlic
salt and black pepper

8 saffron strands
1 egg yolk
¼ pint (150 ml) thick cream
juice of 1 lemon

Preparation 15 minutes
Cooking 3½ hours,
    including cooling

MENU PLANNING: For a special dinner this can be followed by a rich main course, perhaps Chicken Marengo (see page 50).

1. Boil the giblets in a large covered saucepan with 3 pints (1.75 litres) water for 15 minutes, skimming off the scum that rises to the surface.
2. Add the vegetables, garlic, salt, pepper and saffron to the boiling stock and simmer, covered, for 1 hour, removing any further scum.
3. Strain the stock and leave it to cool until the fat can be removed from the surface – this will probably take a couple of hours.*
4. Reheat the stock.
5. Blend the egg yolk, cream and lemon juice in a serving tureen then stir in the hot stock, a little at a time, until it is all mixed in smoothly. Serve at once.

SOPA PICADILLO

Chicken stock, ham, hard-boiled egg and fried croûtons are the usual ingredients for this peasant soup from Andalusia. The soup gets much of its flavour from the stock so you must use a good one. The addition of chick peas makes it a meal in itself, and a leaf of fresh mint floating on each serving adds a perfect additional touch of flavour.

4 ounces (100 g) chick peas, soaked in cold water for 24 hours then drained
1½ pints (900 ml) chicken stock (see page 22)
4 or 5 medium-thick slices of chorizo or other spicy dried sausage
3 tablespoons oil
4 ounces (100 g) crustless white bread, cut into cubes

4 ounces (100 g) cooked ham, chopped
2 hard-boiled eggs, chopped
6 mint leaves

Soaking 24 hours
Preparation 5 minutes
Cooking 1 hour 45 minutes

MENU PLANNING: For a Spanish meal follow with Spanish omelette or our version of a Piperade (see page 75).

1. In a large, covered saucepan, simmer the chick peas in the stock for about 1 hour.
2. Add the chorizo or other sausage, and simmer, covered, for 30 minutes.*
3. Heat the oil and fry the bread cubes, turning frequently until evenly golden brown. Drain on absorbent paper.
4. Stir the ham and hard-boiled eggs into the chick peas and heat through.
5. Float a mint leaf on each serving, then sprinkle on the bread croûtons.

CHICKEN AND PARSNIP SOUP*

We invented this soup when all we had left one Sunday evening were some parsnips and the remains of the chicken we had had for lunch. It could also be made from 3-4 ounces (75-100 g) of any cooked chicken and 1½ pints (900 ml) stock that has been made separately.

the remains of a cooked whole chicken and the giblets and skin, if available
1 ounce (25 g) butter
1½ lb (750 g) parsnips, diced

1 teaspoon brown sugar
salt and black pepper

Preparation 20 minutes
Cooking 1 hour

MENU PLANNING: Makes a simple supper, followed by eggs on toast.

1. Take the meat off the chicken bones and simmer the bones with the skin and giblets, if available, in a large, covered saucepan in just over 1½ pints (900 ml) water for 45 minutes, removing any scum that rises.
2. Chop the chicken meat.
3. Melt the butter in a saucepan and stir in the parsnips, sugar and 2-3 tablespoons of water.
4. Cook gently for 10-15 minutes, adding a little more water if the parsnips start to catch or burn.
5. Stir in the stock, chicken, salt and pepper, bring to the boil and simmer for 5 minutes.

CHICKEN YOGHURT SOUP

A slightly different chicken-flavoured soup that is well worth making.

1 teaspoon cornflour
½ pint (300 ml) plain
  yoghurt
1 pint (600 ml) chicken
  stock (see page 22)
3 egg yolks, beaten
2 tablespoons ground
  almonds

salt and black pepper
½ ounce (15 g) butter
1 tablespoon chopped fresh
  mint

Preparation 5 minutes
Cooking 20 minutes

MENU PLANNING: A delicate soup that goes well with dry sherry.

1. In a small saucepan, mix the cornflour with a little water then gradually stir in the yoghurt.
2. Bring to the boil slowly, stirring all the time, and simmer until thickened.
3. Bring the stock to the boil in a covered saucepan, remove from the heat and allow to cool slightly.
4. Blend a little of the stock with the egg yolks until they are the consistency of thin cream, then stir the 'cream' into the stock.
5. Heat the stock over a low heat, stirring all the time until it thickens. Do not boil or it will curdle.
6. Stir in the yoghurt, ground almonds, salt and pepper.
7. Melt the butter in a small pan, add the mint and heat through. Stir into the soup just before serving.

SIMPLE PÂTÉ

There are numerous chicken liver pâté recipes, but we think this is one of the simplest and best. For variety, four anchovy fillets can be minced in – but reduce the salt. Because the onion is almost raw the pâté should not be kept too long, but do keep it for a few hours before eating, to allow the flavours to mature.

1 pound (450 g) chicken livers
4 anchovy fillets (optional)
8 ounces (225 g) butter
8 ounces (225 g) onions, minced or very finely chopped
1 teaspoon grated nutmeg
1 teaspoon mustard powder

½ teaspoon ground cloves
2 tablespoons sherry
salt and black pepper

Preparation 5 minutes
Cooking 20 minutes
Cooling 2 hours

MENU PLANNING: Serve with white toast. Butter not needed.

1. Poach the chicken livers in a little water for 5 minutes, drain and then mince – with the anchovies, if used.
2. Heat the butter in a small saucepan until it begins to bubble, add the onions and cook for 2 minutes.
3. Stir in the remaining ingredients and when thoroughly mixed transfer to a bowl to cool.

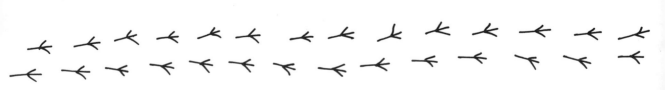

CHICKEN LIVER PÂTÉ

This is another simple chicken liver pâté which needs little cooking. It differs from the previous one chiefly in using no onions.

2½ ounces (65 g) butter
1 pound (450 g) chicken
  livers
3 tablespoons sherry
3 tablespoons brandy
½ teaspoon dried thyme
½ teaspoon dried basil
½ teaspoon dried
  marjoram
¼ teaspoon mixed spice

1 clove of garlic, crushed
salt and black pepper

Preparation none
Cooking 18 minutes

MENU PLANNING: Serve
with wholemeal bread.
Drink white wine.

1. Heat the butter in a frying pan, add the livers and cook lightly – they should remain red inside.
2. Either mash the livers in the pan with the sherry and brandy then thoroughly mix in the remaining ingredients, or mix them all in a blender or food processor.
3. Transfer the pâté to one or more bowls and leave to cool. If keeping for more than a day, cover with melted butter.

TERRINE MAISON

For this you need a 2 pint (1.2 litre) terrine (or casserole) which can be sealed with flour and water paste, i.e. one which has an inner rim on which the lid rests. You will also need a plate or metal disc that will fit inside the terrine for pressing the pâté once it has been cooked.

6 to 8 slices of streaky bacon
12 ounces (350 g) chicken livers
1 small onion
12 ounces (350 g) sausage-meat
2 cloves of garlic
2 hard-boiled eggs, chopped
1 teaspoon each of fresh chopped thyme, parsley
and basil (or ½ teaspoon of each dried herb)
salt and black pepper
12 ounces (350 g) cooked chicken, sliced
2 ounces (50 g) flour

Preparation 20 minutes
Cooking 1½ hours
Temperature 350°F (180°C) gas mark 4
Pressing 12 hours

MENU PLANNING: Serve with pickles and chutneys.

1. Line the terrine with the bacon.
2. Mince the livers, onion, sausage-meat and garlic together.
3. Thoroughly mix in the hard-boiled eggs, herbs, salt and pepper.
4. Place a thin layer of this mixture in the bottom of the terrine followed by a layer of the chicken.
5. Continue adding alternate layers, ending with the minced mixture.
6. Mix the flour to a stiff paste with water then use to seal the terrine.
7. Place the terrine in a roasting tin of hot water and cook for 1½ hours at 350°F (180°C) gas mark 4.
8. Remove the lid and press the terrine with a plate or disc and 2 pound (1 kg) weight. Leave it in a cool place for 12 hours.
9. Remove the weight and plate or disc and invert the terrine on to a serving plate. It should slip out easily, but if it doesn't, hold the plate and terrine firmly together and give a sharp shake.

GEHAKTE LEBER

The essential ingredient of this traditional Jewish chicken liver pâté is rendered down chicken fat. No other fat will do.

4 tablespoons chicken fat
1 pound (450 g) chicken
* livers, sliced*
3 hard-boiled eggs
8 ounces (225 g) onions
salt

Preparation 10 minutes
Cooking 20 minutes
Cooling 2 hours

MENU PLANNING: Serve with light rye bread or unleavened bread (matzo).

1. Heat 2 tablespoons chicken fat in a frying pan, add the livers and fry gently for about 4 minutes – the liver should remain pink inside.
2. Mince the liver with 1½ hard-boiled eggs.
3. Fry the onion in the remaining fat over a moderate heat until soft and slightly coloured.
4. Mix the onion with the liver, add the salt and transfer to a dish to cool.
5. Separate and chop the yolks and whites of the remaining hard-boiled eggs. Decorate the edge of the pâté with the white, the centre with the yolk.

PÂTÉ-TERRINE DE VOLAILLE

An oval 2 pint (1.2 litre) terrine is in theory best for this dish, but in practice the boned chicken can be made to fit quite tightly enough into a round one. The brandy is *not* optional, though it need not be a distinguished one and Grappa or Marc are legitimate substitutes.

the chicken's liver and heart, finely chopped
8 ounces (225 g) minced veal
8 ounces (225 g) minced pork
2 slices of dry bread soaked in 2 fluid ounces (50 ml) milk
8 juniper berries, crushed
2 cloves of garlic, crushed
salt and black pepper
3½-4 lb (1.5-1.75 kg) roasting chicken, boned (see method B on page 15)
8 ounces (225 g) thinly sliced ham

8 ounces (225 g) lean veal, thinly sliced
4 thin slices of streaky bacon
2 bay leaves
2 sprigs of fresh thyme or 1 teaspoon dried thyme
¼ pint (150 ml) brandy
2 ounces (50 g) flour

Preparation 1½ hours
Cooking 2½ hours
Temperature 300°F (150°C) gas mark 2
Cooling 3 hours

MENU PLANNING: Serve with toast.

1. Mix the chicken's liver and and heart with the minced veal, pork, bread and milk, juniper berries, garlic and salt and pepper.
2. Place a layer of this mixture over the exposed flesh of the chicken, pushing it well into the spaces left by the thigh bones.
3. Cover with layers of ham and sliced veal, then add more of the stuffing mixture and continue in this way until all are used.
4. Reassemble the chicken and sew it up along its back.
5. Line the bottom of the terrine with 2 slices of bacon, then add a bay leaf and a sprig of thyme and place the chicken on top.
6. Pour on the brandy and sufficient water to fill the spaces between the chicken and the sides of the terrine.

7. Top with the other bay leaf and sprig of thyme and the remaining bacon.
8. Mix the flour to a stiff paste with water and use to seal the terrine. Cook for 2½ hours at 300°F (150°C) gas mark 2. Leave to cool before opening.

CROSTINI

This Tuscan speciality is usually served before the main course. We have often eaten crostini in Italy, but frankly have never tasted any better than the ones we make at home.

3-4 ounces (75-100 g) butter
2 ounces (50 g) ham, diced
8 ounces (225 g) chicken livers, chopped
1 tablespoon flour
½ teaspoon lemon juice

2 tablespoons chicken stock (see page 22)
salt and black pepper
10-12 slices of French bread

Preparation 5 minutes
Cooking 20 minutes

MENU PLANNING: No accompaniment needed except Tuscan red wine, say Chianti.

1. Melt 1 ounce (25 g) butter in a small pan, add the ham and fry gently for 2 minutes.
2. Coat the livers in flour, add to the ham and cook over a low heat for 3-4 minutes. Pour on the lemon juice and stock and add the seasoning. Cover and cook for a further 10 minutes.
3. Meanwhile, melt the remaining butter in a frying pan and fry the bread until brown and crisp.
4. Spread the hot chicken liver mixture on the fried bread and serve.

CURRIED FRITOS

To make these small Spanish rissoles look really elegant, make the stuffing quite stiff and deep fry them. Otherwise use plenty of hot fat in a shallow frying pan. The filling can be prepared in advance.

For the filling
oil
8 ounces (225 g) onions, minced
2 teaspoons medium-strength curry powder
3 tomatoes, peeled and chopped
3 fluid ounces (75 ml) chicken stock (see page 22)
salt
6-8 ounces (175-225 g) cooked chicken, minced
oil for frying

For the batter
4 ounces (100 g) flour
1 tablespoon oil
6 fluid ounces (175 ml) chicken stock (see page 22)
salt and white pepper
2 egg whites, whisked

Preparation 30 minutes
Cooling and chilling at least 1½ hours
Cooking 15 minutes

MENU PLANNING: Serve on their own.
Drink a dry white Spanish wine.

1. For the filling, heat the oil in a large frying pan, add the onions and cook until soft.
2. Stir in the curry powder, tomatoes, stock and salt and simmer until reduced to a thick purée.
3. Stir in the chicken. Leave to cool, then spread out on a plate and leave in the refrigerator to chill thoroughly. Make into small, walnut-sized balls.
4. For the batter, blend the flour and oil together then stir in the stock, salt and pepper. Fold in the egg whites.

5. Coat the chicken balls with the batter. Lower a few balls at a time into hot oil and cook quickly until evenly browned and crisp. Remove from the oil and drain on absorbent paper. Continue in this way until all the balls have been cooked. Check the temperature of the oil occasionally.
6. Serve hot.

CREAM CHEESE MOUSSE

Our friend Ruby Coghlan invented this featherlight chicken mousse. A blender or food processor is needed to get the smooth texture.

4 chicken thighs
8 ounces (225 g) cream cheese
4 tablespoons mayonnaise
1 packet (approximately 0.85 ounces [22 g]) aspic powder
salt and black pepper
For the marinade
4 fluid ounces (100 ml) dry white wine
white pepper

1 clove of garlic, crushed
1 tablespoon olive oil
1 sprig of fresh rosemary or ½ teaspoon dried rosemary
1 sprig of fresh thyme or ¼ teaspoon dried thyme

Marinating 24 hours
Preparation none
Cooking 40 minutes
Cooling 6 hours

MENU PLANNING: Serve with thin slices of toast as an hors d'oeuvre, or with a salad for a light lunch.

1. Whisk all the ingredients for the marinade together. Put the chicken thighs into a dish which they will just fit, pour the marinade over, cover and leave in the refrigerator for 24 hours, turning the thighs over occasionally.

2. Put the chicken in a saucepan with the marinade and 3 fluid ounces (75 ml) water and simmer, covered, until tender – about 25 minutes.

3. Strain off and reserve the liquid. Remove the flesh from the bones and put into a blender or food processor with the skin, reserved liquid, cream cheese and mayonnaise. Blend until smooth.

4. Dissolve the aspic powder in ½ pint (300 ml) boiling water and add about 6 tablespoons to the chicken mixture.

5. Blend briefly to mix. Taste and season, if necessary.

6. Pour into a shallow serving dish and cover with the remaining aspic. Before pouring the aspic over it is very effective to make an arrangement of, for instance, bay leaves, which will set in the jelly.

41

TERRINE WITH PORK*

You can mince belly of pork yourself for this otherwise simple and tasty terrine, but it is a stringy business unless you have a power mincer, so we usually buy ready-minced pork.

1 pound (450 g) minced
  pork
½ pint (300 ml) wine, red
  or white
8 ounces (225 g) chicken
  livers, sliced
1 large onion, finely
  chopped
2 cloves of garlic, crushed
1 teaspoon fresh thyme or
  ½ teaspoon dried thyme
¼ teaspoon mustard
  powder

1 egg
salt and black pepper
4 cloves
4 bay leaves
3 slices of streaky bacon

Marinading 12 hours
Preparation 10 minutes
Cooking 1¾ hours
Temperature 300°F
  (150°C) gas mark 2
Cooling 3 hours

MENU PLANNING: Serve with toast and fresh lettuce leaves.

1. Marinate the pork in the wine for 12 hours.
2. Gently poach the chicken livers in a little water for about 3 minutes then mince them.
3. Drain the pork, reserving the marinade, and mix with the livers, onion, garlic, thyme, mustard, egg, seasoning and sufficient of the marinade to produce a moist, but not too soft, consistency.
4. Put into an oven-proof dish with a capacity of about 2 pints (1.2 litres) and with upright sides and top with the cloves and bay leaves followed by the bacon rashers.
5. Place the dish in a pan of hot water and cook uncovered, in the oven for about 1½ hours at 300°F (150°C) gas mark 2. The terrine is ready when it has shrunk from the sides of the dish.
6. Allow to cool, shake to loosen it on all sides, turn it out on to one hand, then reverse it on to a plate.

CHICKEN BEDSPRINGS

This was invented by Jessica, Cordelia's youngest sister, and consists of a combination of boned and gently fried chicken, pasta spirals and a strongly flavoured herb sauce in which sage and rosemary predominate.

3 tablespoons olive oil
flesh from a 3½-4 lb (1.5-
1.75 kg) roasting chicken,
chopped into 1-1½ inch
(2.5-4 cm) pieces
12 ounces (350 g) pasta
spirals
salt

For the sauce
2 tablespoons tomato purée
6-8 tablespoons olive oil
1 clove of garlic, crushed
2-3 ounces (50-75 g) mixed
fresh sage, rosemary,
marjoram, thyme and
chives, finely chopped

Preparation 30 minutes
Cooking 25 minutes

MENU PLANNING: Serve with fennel baked with Parmesan cheese. Drink Chianti.

1. Heat the oil in a large frying pan and fry the chicken, turning once or twice, until tender – about 8 minutes.
2. Meanwhile, boil the pasta in plenty of salted water, plus a few drops of oil to keep the pieces separate, until just tender – about 12-14 minutes.
3. For the sauce, simmer the tomato purée, oil, garlic and herbs together gently for 5 minutes.
4. Drain the pasta, place in a warmed dish and put the chicken on top.
5. Add the cooking juices from the chicken to the sauce, reheat and pour over the chicken and pasta.

PILAU, CAPE STYLE

Our South African friend, Hansell Hewitt, introduced us to this pilau, which comes from *Cape Cookery: Simple Yet Distinctive,* published in 1890 by his great uncle, and which he claims was the first South African cookery book. Our version uses less than half as much butter.

3½ lb (1.5 kg) roasting chicken, cut into 12 pieces (see page 13)
the chicken's skin and giblets
1 onion, sliced
2 blades of mace
1 clove
bunch of fresh parsley
salt and black pepper
¼ pint (150 ml) milk
1 tablespoon flour

1 ounce (25 g) butter
For the rice
12 ounces (350 g) long-grain rice
1 ounce (25 g) butter
1 teaspoon allspice
salt and black pepper
For the garnish
1 hard-boiled egg, chopped

Preparation 15 minutes
Stock 1 hour
Cooking 50 minutes

MENU PLANNING: Serve with watercress or endive salad.
Drink a dry red South African wine.

1. In a covered saucepan simmer the feet, neck, gizzard, heart, wing tips and skin of the chicken in 1 pint (600 ml) water with the onion, blades of mace, clove, parsley, salt and pepper for 1 hour.
2. Strain the stock and return to the pan. Gradually blend the milk into the flour, then add to the stock.
3. Add the butter and chicken, cover and simmer until tender – about 30 minutes.*
4. Remove the chicken and keep warm.
5. Boil the liquor until reduced to a thick purée.
6. For the rice, melt the butter in a large saucepan, add the rice and cook, stirring, until it becomes translucent then stir in 1½ times its volume of water Bring to the boil, cover and simmer for 12-14 minutes until the rice is just tender and the liquid is absorbed. Stir in the allspice, salt and pepper.
7. Make a bed of the rice on a warmed large flat dish, put the chicken on top and pour the reduced stock over. Garnish with the hard-boiled egg.

CRISP AND SMOOTH

Once you get the hang of this quick and easy recipe it will only take about 15 minutes in all. The result is a delicious combination of tastes and textures.

1 tablespoon oil
8 ounces (225 g) chicken livers, roughly chopped
1 lb (450 g) bean shoots
2-3 cloves of garlic,

crushed
salt and black pepper

Preparation 5 minutes
Cooking 10 minutes

MENU PLANNING: Serve with a tomato salad. Drink dry red or white *vin ordinaire*.

1. Heat the oil in a large frying pan or a wok, add the livers and fry, stirring frequently, for 5 minutes.
2. Add the bean shoots, stir well, then add the garlic and a generous amount of salt and pepper.
3. Cook for 4-5 minutes then serve.

CANTONESE CHICKEN

This dish is as easy, and almost as quick, as the previous one.

1 ounce (25 g) butter
1 tablespoon olive oil
2 medium carrots, thinly sliced
1 green pepper, thinly sliced
8 ounces (225 g) bean shoots

6 ounces (175 g) chicken, diced
2 tablespoons soy sauce
salt

Preparation 20 minutes
Cooking 10 minutes

MENU PLANNING: Serve with brown rice and spring onions. Drink white *vin ordinaire*.

1. Heat the butter and oil in a heavy pan or a wok, add the carrots and pepper and fry briskly for 2 minutes.
2. Add the bean shoots, chicken and soy sauce and cook over a moderate heat for 5 minutes.
3. Taste for salt and serve at once.

CHICKEN LIVERS MADEIRA

Kidneys and liver blend together excellently in this simple and effective Greek dish.

3 ounces (75 g) butter
6 lambs' kidneys, halved, cored and cut into ½-¾ inch (1.25-4 cm) pieces
1 lb (450 g) chicken livers
1 ounce (25 g) flour
1 small onion, finely chopped
2 cloves of garlic, crushed
1 tablespoon chopped fresh parsley

1 teaspoon lemon juice
½ pint (300 ml) chicken stock (see page 22)
salt and black pepper
4 fluid ounces (100 ml) Madeira

Preparation 15 minutes
Cooking 15 minutes

MENU PLANNING: Serve with mashed potatoes or rice and baked tomatoes. Drink Retsina, or a non-resinated dry white Greek wine.

1. Heat the butter in a large frying pan, add the kidneys and livers and fry over a high heat for 4 minutes, stirring all the time to prevent burning.
2. Sprinkle in the flour and continue to cook over a high heat for 1-2 minutes until it browns.
3. Remove the livers and kidneys and keep warm.
4. Add the onion, garlic, parsley and lemon juice then gradually stir in the stock. Continue heating, stirring constantly, until it bubbles again then simmer for 5 minutes.
5. Season, then stir in the Madeira.
6. Return the liver and kidney to the pan and reheat.

PARMESAN CHICKEN

There are many different coatings for fried chicken, but we think lemon and Parmesan cheese is the most delicious. Use the chicken breast, cut into four pieces, the thighs and the drumsticks. The other joints can be used for a risotto (see pages 117, 120) or Paella (see page 89).

3½-4 lb (1.5-1.75 kg)
  roasting chicken, jointed
  (see page 13)
2 ounces (50 g) flour
salt and black pepper
2-3 ounces (50-75 g) fresh
  breadcrumbs

1 ounce (25 g) grated
  Parmesan cheese
zest of 1 lemon
1 egg, whisked
3 tablespoons oil

Preparation 20 minutes
Cooking 30 minutes

MENU PLANNING: Serve as a chicken Maryland with fried bananas, corn fritters and baked tomatoes.
Drink a light white wine, say a Moselle.

1. Coat the chicken in the flour seasoned with salt and pepper.
2. Mix the breadcrumbs, cheese and lemon zest together.
3. Brush the chicken pieces with the egg then coat in the breadcrumb mixture.
4. Heat the oil in a large frying pan, add the chicken and fry until tender – about 30 minutes. Wait until well browned before turning for the first time or the coating may become detached. Drain on absorbent paper before serving.

LEMON AND ORANGE CHICKEN

It's less easy than you might think to give a roast chicken a lemon or orange flavour, but with the method we've devised the citrus flavour really gets into the chicken flesh. You can use an orange and a lemon, as we suggest, or you could use two of either.

1 orange
1 lemon
1 ounce (25 g) butter,
  softened
3½-4 lb (1.5-1.75 kg)
  roasting chicken
salt and pepper

Preparation 15 minutes
Cooking 1½ hours
Temperature 350°F
  (180°C) gas mark 4

MENU PLANNING: Serve with noodles and mushrooms. Drink a dry white wine, say from the Loire.

1. Grate the zest from the orange and lemon and mix with the butter.
2. Squeeze the juice from the orange and lemon.
3. Make a 1-2 inch (2.5-5 cm) slit in the skin of the chicken down the line of the breastbone, slip your fingers under the skin and ease it away from the breast. Insert the zest and butter mixture, forcing it well down on both sides. Pour in the juices.
4. Put the squeezed lemon and orange halves into the bird's cavity. Close with a skewer – there is no need to sew it.
5. Season the outside of the bird, then roast in a chicken brick, covered roasting tin or wrapped in foil for 1½ hours at 350°F (180°C) gas mark 4.
6. Skim the fat from the cooking juices and serve them as a sauce.

CHICKEN MARENGO*

Napoleon's cook is supposed to have invented the original dish in northern Italy when the only things he could scrounge were farmyard chickens and wild mushrooms. Apricots are our addition.

2 ounces (50 g) butter
3½-4 lb (1.5-1.75 kg)
  roasting chicken, jointed
  (see page 13)
½ pint (300 ml) white wine
6 tomatoes, peeled and
  chopped, or 14 ounce
  (400 g) can of tomatoes
4 ounces (100 g)
  mushrooms
2 cloves of garlic, crushed
1 chicken stock cube,
  crumbled

2 ounces (50 g) chopped
  dried apricots, optional
bouquet garni of a bay leaf,
  sprig of parsley and sprig
  of thyme
1 tablespoon flour

Preparation 15 minutes
Cooking 1 hour 15 minutes
Temperature 350°F
  (180°C) gas mark 4

MENU PLANNING: Serve with potatoes boiled in their skins and a tomato and fennel salad.
Drink a dry white wine, say Soave.

1. Heat the butter in a large frying pan and fry the chicken until browned.
2. Transfer to an oven-proof casserole with the frying juices and add all other ingredients, except flour.
3. Cover and cook for 45 minutes at 350°F (180°C) gas mark 4.
4. Gradually blend the flour with a little of the liquid then stir into the casserole and cook for 15 minutes.

CHICKEN AND CRAB

Chicken and seafood make a surprisingly good combination: you can also use shrimps or prawns for this recipe. The drumsticks can be prepared in advance and will taste even better if cooked over a wood fire or a barbecue. These quantities are for four – at two drumsticks each.

6 ounces (175 g) flaked
  crab meat
1½ ounces (40 g) butter
juice and grated zest
  of ½ a lemon
1 tablespoon chopped fresh
  parsley or 1½ teaspoons
  dried parsley
salt and black pepper

8 chicken drumsticks
For the baste
5 tablespoons olive oil
juice of 1 lemon
1 clove of garlic, crushed

Preparation 20 minutes
Chilling 30 minutes
Cooking 20-30 minutes

MENU PLANNING: Serve with jacket potatoes and cucumber and yoghurt salad. Drink white wine.

1. Mash the crab with the butter, lemon juice and zest, parsley, salt and pepper.
2. Lift the skin of the drumsticks and slice the flesh lengthways to make room for the crab mixture.
3. Push the crab mixture under the skin of the drumsticks and into the slit in the flesh. Cover with the skin. Chill for at least 30 minutes.
4. For the baste, stir the oil, lemon juice and garlic together.
5. Cook the drumsticks under a moderately hot grill, or on a grid over an open fire, basting frequently, for 10-15 minutes on each side, cooking the stuffed side first.

WEST AFRICAN PEANUT STEW*

You can make this traditional West African stew as hot as you like by adding more or less cayenne pepper. Use crunchy peanut butter, for preference a brand to which sugar has *not* been added.

oil for frying
2 onions, chopped
2 green peppers, chopped
3½-4 lb (1.5-1.75 kg)
  roasting chicken, jointed
  (see page 13)
6 ounces (175 g) crunchy
  peanut butter
2 ounces (50 g) peanuts,
  chopped
1 tablespoon vinegar
2 tablespoons tomato purée

½ teaspoon cayenne pepper
¼ teaspoon ground cumin
salt
approximately 1 pint
  (600 ml) chicken stock
  (see page 22)

Preparation 15 minutes
Cooking 3 hours
Temperature 225°F
  (110°C) gas mark ¼

MENU PLANNING: Serve with baked sweet potatoes. Drink beer.

1. Heat the oil in a frying pan, add the onions and peppers and cook slowly until soft.
2. Transfer to an oven-proof casserole with a slotted spoon then fry the chicken in the frying pan until evenly browned.
3. Add to the casserole with the remaining ingredients, pouring in just enough stock to almost cover them. Stir to distribute the peanut butter.
4. Cover and cook for 2½ hours at 225°F (110°C) gas mark ¼, or at the lowest temperature at which your oven functions efficiently.

NORMANDY CHICKEN

Apples, onions and cream abound in Normandy. This casserole uses the cream and the apples, both raw and in the form of apple brandy – calvados. The cinnamon is our own addition.

3 ounces (75 g) butter
6 dessert apples, cored, skinned and chopped
1 teaspoon ground cinnamon
3½-4 lb (1.5-1.75 kg) roasting chicken
¼ pint (150 ml) thin cream
2 tablespoons calvados

salt and pepper

Preparation 10 minutes
Cooking 1 hour 30 minutes
Temperature 350°F (180°C) gas mark 4

MENU PLANNING: Serve with jacket potatoes. Drink cider.

1. Heat the butter in a frying pan and lightly fry the apples, sprinkling them with cinnamon as they cook. Remove with a slotted spoon.
2. Fry the chicken in the same pan until evenly browned.
3. Put some of the apples into an oven-proof casserole, place the chicken on top, then pack the remaining apples around and pour on half the cream.
4. Cover and cook for 1 hour at 350°F (180°C) gas mark 4, turning the chicken over half way through.
5. Transfer the chicken to a warmed serving plate. Stir the remaining cream and the calvados into the apples, taste for seasoning and heat through, but do not boil. Serve as a sauce.

NAIROBI CURRY

We learned this simple curry from Salim Yakub, owner of a Nairobi garage, later a member of Kenya's legislative council. It needed to be simple because Salim and his friends would buy the chickens live in the market on their way into the country and kill, pluck, skin and cook the birds at the picnic spot, refreshing themselves with large whiskies as they worked. All was cooked over a wood fire.

3½-4 lb (1.5-1.75 kg)
  roasting chicken, skinned
  and jointed (see page 13)
chicken skin and giblets
2 medium onions, chopped
1 green pepper, chopped
4 dried red chillies
salt

1 teaspoon turmeric
½ teaspoon ground cloves
1 teaspoon ground ginger
2 tablespoons tomato purée

Preparation 15 minutes
Cooking 1 hour 45 minutes

MENU PLANNING: Serve with rice.
Drink well-watered Scotch or lager.

1. In a covered saucepan, simmer the chicken skin and giblets in just under 1 pint (500 ml) water for 30 minutes.
2. Remove the skin and giblets, add the chicken, onions, pepper, salt and chillies and cover and simmer for 30 minutes.
3. Add the turmeric, cloves, ginger and tomato purée and simmer, covered, for another 45 minutes.

SOUTHERN FRIED CHICKEN

This is an easy way of achieving the characteristic rich, slightly sweet taste of the cooking of the southern United States of America. The cooking time may seem long but this is needed to reduce the sauce and allow it to coat and penetrate the meat.

3½-4 lb (1.5-1.75 kg) roasting chicken, jointed (see page 13)
salt and black pepper
3 tablespoons oil
8 ounces (225 g) butter
3 tablespoons Worcestershire sauce
2 tablespoons tomato purée
1 teaspoon brown sugar or honey

2 teaspoons lemon juice or vinegar
1-3 dried chillies

Preparation 15 minutes
Cooking 1 hour 15 minutes
Temperature 350°F (180°C) gas mark 4

MENU PLANNING: Serve with corn bread and a green salad.
Drink lager.

1. Season the chicken with salt and pepper.
2. Heat the oil in a frying pan, add the chicken and fry until lightly browned on both sides.
3. Melt the butter in a small saucepan and stir in the remaining ingredients plus ¼ pint (150 ml) water.
4. Put the chicken into an oven-proof casserole, pour the sauce over and cook for 45 minutes, basting occasionally, at 350°F (180°C) gas mark 4.
5. Remove the chicken from the casserole. Skim some of the surface fat from the juices before serving them spooned over the chicken.

POLLO VERDE

This is a dish which really does seem to be made more delicious by its appearance. The sauce uses elements from two Italian sauces, *salsa verde* and *pesto genovese*, and is a brilliant green. Three ounces (75 g) of fresh herbs may seem a large amount but do not use less.

For the sauce
juice of 1 lemon
10 tablespoons olive oil
2 cloves of garlic
3 ounces (75 g) fresh basil, marjoram, mint or parsley in the proportions you fancy.
3 teaspoons capers.
1½ ounces (40 g) grated Parmesan cheese

3½-4 lb (1.5-1.75 kg) roasting chicken, jointed (see page 13)
olive oil
salt and black pepper
For serving
2 tablespoons pine nuts

Preparation 15 minutes
Cooking 45 minutes
Temperature 350°F (180°C) gas mark 4

MENU PLANNING: Serve with courgettes and creamy mashed potatoes or noodles. Drink a white Italian wine, say Orvieto.

1. For the sauce, mix all the ingredients together in a blender or liquidiser.
2. Rub the chicken with olive oil, sprinkle with salt and pepper, put in an oven-proof dish and cook, covered, for 45 minutes at 350°F (180°C) gas mark 4.
3. Serve the individual joints of chicken topped with ample green sauce and sprinkled with pine nuts.

FARMHOUSE ROAST CHICKEN

A simple French way to roast chicken – but just right.

3½-4 lb (1.5-1.75 kg) roasting chicken
4-5 slices of salt pork or smoked bacon
1 ounce (25 g) butter

Preparation 5 minutes
Cooking 1 hour 25 minutes - 1 hour 35 minutes
Temperature 375°F (190°C) gas mark 5

MENU PLANNING: Serve with roast potatoes and roast parsnips. Drink Burgundy, claret or a red *vin ordinaire*.

1. Cover the chicken with the pork or bacon, tying them in place if necessary.
2. Place in a baking tin with ¼ pint (150 ml) of water and 1 ounce (25 g) of butter.
3. Roast for 1 hour 25 minutes-1 hour 35 minutes at 375°F (190°C) gas mark 5, basting every ten minutes.

4. Transfer the chicken to a warmed serving dish and keep warm. Discard the salt pork or bacon.
5. Pour off excess fat from the baking tin, add ½ pint (300 ml) water and boil, stirring to dislodge the sediment until reduced. Serve as gravy.

MUSHROOM CASSEROLE

If you cook the mushrooms separately as we suggest, they retain their own flavour and give distinction to this otherwise simple casserole.

*3½-4 lb (1.5-1.75 kg)
  roasting chicken, jointed
  (see page 13)
2 ounces (50 g) salted flour
3 tablespoons oil
3 tomatoes, peeled and
  chopped
¼ pint (150 ml) dry white
  wine*

*1 tablespoon fresh thyme
  or 1 teaspoon dried thyme
1 ounce (25 g) butter
8 ounces (225 g)
  mushrooms, chopped
2 cloves of garlic, crushed
salt and black pepper*

*Preparation 10 minutes
Cooking 45 minutes*

MENU PLANNING: Serve with sautéed potatoes and braised celery.
Drink a white *vin ordinaire*.

1. Coat the chicken joints in salted flour.
2. Heat the oil in a large frying pan, add the chicken and cook until golden brown then transfer to a casserole.
3. Add the tomatoes, wine and thyme, cover and simmer until tender – about 30 minutes. If there is too much liquid, remove the lid and let it reduce.*
4. Meanwhile, melt the butter in a small, heavy pan, add the mushrooms and garlic and cook gently for 2-3 minutes.
5. Stir the mushrooms and their cooking juices into the chicken. Taste for seasoning.

POUSSIN WITH SOUR CREAM

Any young chicken can be grilled but poussins are best because they need the least cooking. The delicate flavour of the sour cream sauce exactly complements and enhances the flavour of the chicken.

3 poussins, cut in half
  through the breast
olive oil
For the sauce
½ pint (300 ml) sour
  cream

1 egg yolk
salt and black pepper

Preparation 15 minutes
Cooking 35 minutes

MENU PLANNING: Serve with peas and sautéed mushrooms.
Drink a young light red wine, say Beaujolais.

1. Run a skewer through the wing and leg of each poussin half to keep it flat.
2. Rub the poussins with plenty of olive oil.
3. Place the poussins under a hot grill and brown quickly for a couple of minutes on each side.
4. Lower the heat and continue to cook for about 25 minutes, turning them occasionally, until the flesh is tender.
5. For the sauce, blend the sour cream with the egg yolk, then cook in a double saucepan or bowl placed over a pan of hot water, stirring constantly, until the sauce thickens slightly. Add the seasoning.
6. Serve with the sauce poured over the poussins.

SAUTÉ À LA PAYSANNE

This is a splendidly sustaining peasant casserole, ideal for a cold winter day.

4 ounces (100 g) butter
2 lb (1 kg) potatoes, peeled and cut into ½-¾ inch (1.2-2 cm) cubes
3½-4 lb (1.5-1.75 kg) roasting chicken, jointed (see page 13)
¼ pint (150 ml) dry white wine
3 fluid ounces (75 ml) chicken stock (see page 22)

2 bay leaves
1 tablespoon fresh parsley, chopped or 1 teaspoon dried parsley
salt and black pepper

Preparation 15 minutes
Cooking 1 hour 10 minutes
Temperature 350°F (180°C) gas mark 4

MENU PLANNING: Serve with steamed cabbage and leeks.
Drink a red *vin ordinaire*.

1. Heat 1 ounce (25 g) butter in a heavy pan, add the potatoes and cook for 2-3 minutes.
2. Fry the chicken in the remaining butter in a heavy oven-proof casserole until evenly browned.
3. Add the potatoes to the chicken, cover and cook for 45 minutes at 350°F (180°C) gas mark 4.
4. Remove the chicken and potatoes and keep warm on a serving dish.
5. Stir the remaining ingredients into the cooking juices and boil, uncovered, for about 10 minutes until reduced.
6. Remove the bay leaves, taste for seasoning then pour the sauce over the chicken and potatoes.

CHICKEN FRICASSÉE

In this recipe the chicken can really be tasted as there are no spices, except a little pepper, and no garlic to mask its flavour.

1 ounce (25 g) butter
2 tablespoons flour
3½-4 lb (1.5-1.75 kg)
  roasting chicken, skinned
  and jointed (see page 13)
12 small onions, chopped
2 bay leaves
2 sprigs of fresh thyme or
  1 teaspoon of dried thyme
2 stalks of fresh parsley or
  1 teaspoon of dried
  parsley

salt and black pepper
8 ounces (225 g)
  mushrooms, sliced if
  necessary
2 egg yolks, beaten
1 teaspoon lemon juice

Preparation 5 minutes
Cooking 1 hour 25-30
  minutes

MENU PLANNING: Serve with rice and French beans. Drink Chablis or a dry white Bordeaux.

1. Melt the butter in a large heavy pan then stir in the flour.
2. Slowly stir in 1¼ pints (750 ml) water and cook, stirring constantly, until it thickens.
3. Add the chicken, onions, bay leaves, thyme, parsley, salt and pepper, and simmer, covered, for 1 hour, stirring occasionally to make sure that the joints cook evenly.
4. Add the mushrooms and cook for 5 minutes.
5. Transfer the chicken to a warmed serving dish, place the onions and mushrooms around it and keep warm.
6. Strain the sauce, return it to the pan and boil until reduced by half.
7. Blend the egg yolks with a little of the sauce to make a thin cream, then stir the cream into the sauce. Cook over a low heat, stirring constantly, until the sauce thickens. Do not boil.
8. Add the lemon juice and reheat gently but do not boil. Pour some of the sauce over the chicken and serve the rest separately.

GALLINA EN PEPITORIA

This is based on a recipe from the Palace Hotel, Madrid. Marinating the hen, adding green olives and reducing the sauce in the way given are our own modifications.

5 lb (2.25 kg) boiling fowl, skinned and jointed (see page 13)
½ pint (300 ml) dry white wine
2 tablespoons olive oil
1 onion, sliced
2 bay leaves
salt and black pepper
½ pint (300 ml) chicken stock (see page 22)
2 ounces (50 g) flaked almonds
1 teaspoon fresh thyme or ½ teaspoon dried thyme

4 cloves of garlic, crushed
6 green olives, stoned
For the garnish
2 tablespoons oil
2 ounces (50 g) fresh breadcrumbs
1 tablespoon chopped fresh parsley or 1½ teaspoons dried parsley
1 hard-boiled egg, chopped

Marinating 3 hours
Preparation 15 minutes
Cooking 2 hours 30 minutes

MENU PLANNING: Serve with mashed potatoes and boiled baby turnips. Drink a robust red Spanish wine, say from La Mancha.

1. Marinate the chicken in the wine for at least 3 hours, turning the pieces over several times.
2. Drain the joints and pat them dry. Heat the oil in a large, heavy-based pan and fry the chicken until lightly browned then remove the joints with a slotted spoon and keep warm.
3. Fry the onion in the same pan till soft. Replace the chicken, add the bay leaves, salt and pepper, the marinade and enough stock to just cover.
4. Cover and simmer for 1½ hours.
5. Add the almonds, thyme, garlic and olives and a little more stock if necessary. Cover and cook until tender – about 30 minutes.*
6. Transfer the chicken to a warmed serving dish and keep warm.
7. Discard the bay leaves and boil the sauce until reduced to about ½ pint (300 ml).
8. For the garnish, heat the oil in a frying pan, add the breadcrumbs and fry until crisp. Drain well on absorbent paper.
9. Pour the sauce over the chicken and sprinkle on the breadcrumbs, parsley and hard-boiled egg.

MIZUTAKI

A small heater that can be placed on the table is useful for this Japanese dish, or you can finish cooking in the kitchen then keep the dish warm over a candle heater on the table. A heavy and preferably short-handled pan is also necessary. Chicken Mizutaki should be eaten with chopsticks.

For the sauce
2 fluid ounces (50 ml) rice wine or dry sherry
2 fluid ounces (50 ml) soy sauce
1½ fluid ounces (40 ml) lemon juice

flesh from 3½-4 lb (1.5-1.75 kg) roasting chicken cut into 1 inch (2.5 cm) pieces
skin and bones from the chicken
1 onion
8-12 spring onions, diced

bunch of watercress, chopped
4 ounces (100 g) carrots, cut into 1 inch (2.5 cm) pieces
4 ounces (100 g) mushrooms, cut into 1 inch (2.5 cm) pieces
1 green pepper, cut into 1 inch (2.5 cm) pieces

Preparation 40 minutes
Cooking 1 hour 40 minutes

MENU PLANNING: Serve with bowls of boiled rice. Drink hot saki

1. For the sauce, mix all the ingredients together and pour into a small bowl.
2. Simmer the chicken skin and bones in 1½ pints (900 ml) water for 30 minutes.
3. Remove the skin and bones, add the chicken and onion and simmer gently for 35 minutes.
4. Take to the table and place on a low heat.
5. Add the vegetables and heat for 5 minutes.
6. To eat chicken Mizutaki, take out pieces of chicken and vegetable, dip them in the sauce then transfer them to your mouth or to a bed of cooked rice on your plate.
7. Finally, use the remaining sauce, cooking juice and vegetables to make a soup which can be eaten as the conclusion to the meal or kept for another occasion.

WATERZOOI

This recipe is simple except for the final mixing in of the egg yolks, which must be done with extreme care or the sauce will be like scrambled eggs.

1½ ounces (40 g) butter
3 carrots cut into thin strips 1½ inches (4 cm) long
3 sticks of celery, cut into thin strips 1½ inches (4 cm) long
1 onion cut into thin strips 1½ inches (4 cm) long
2-3 leeks cut into thin strips 1½ inches (4 cm) long
2½ lb (1.25 kg) roasting chicken, jointed (see page 13)
½ pint (300 ml) dry white wine or vermouth
¾ pint (450 ml) chicken stock (see page 22)

½ teaspoon fresh tarragon or ¼ teaspoon dried tarragon
2 sprigs of fresh thyme or ½ teaspoon dried thyme
4 sprigs of fresh parsley or 1 tablespoon dried parsley
salt and black pepper
6 egg yolks
¼ pint (150 ml) thick cream
For the garnish
chopped parsley

Preparation 30 minutes
Cooking 1 hour 30 minutes

MENU PLANNING: Serve with sautéed potatoes and more buttered leeks or carrots.
Drink an Alsatian Sylvaner.

1. Melt the butter in a large flame-proof casserole, add the vegetables and cook gently for 10 minutes.
2. Push the vegetables to the sides of the casserole, put in the chicken and cook gently for 10 minutes.
3. Pour in the wine or vermouth and sufficient stock to cover the chicken. Add the herbs, salt and pepper, cover and simmer gently for 35 to 40 minutes.*
4. Pour off the cooking juices and boil in a separate saucepan for a few minutes until reduced to about ¼ pint (150 ml).
5. Blend the egg yolks and cream together then very gradually stir in the reduced juices. Pour over the chicken and vegetables and heat gently, stirring constantly, until the sauce becomes thick and creamy. Do not let it boil.
6. Sprinkle with parsley.

CINNAMON CHICKEN

This dish seems to have been in the family for years. Cinnamon sticks make it look exotic, but ground cinnamon works just as well. You can do more or less the same thing with the individual chicken joints wrapped in foil, but it is not too easy to contain the wine.

3½-4 lb (1.5-1.75 kg) roasting chicken, jointed (see page 13)
3 tablespoons oil
4 tomatoes, peeled and chopped
3 cloves of garlic, crushed
3 cinnamon sticks, roughly crumbled, or 2 teaspoons ground cinnamon

2 ounces (50 g) black olives, stoned
1 orange, cut into 6 or 8 slices
1 lemon, cut into 6 or 8 slices
¼ pint (150 ml) dry white wine
salt and black pepper

Preparation 20 minutes
Cooking 1 hour
Temperature 375°F (190°C) gas mark 5

MENU PLANNING: Serve with fried aubergines and yoghurt.
Drink a red Greek wine, say Demestica.

1. Put the chicken into a heavy oven-proof casserole and pour 1 teaspoon oil over each joint.
2. Place the tomatoes around the chicken. Scatter the garlic, cinnamon and olives over the chicken and place a slice of orange and a slice of lemon on each joint.
3. Pour on the wine and season with salt and pepper.
4. Cover and cook for 1 hour at 375°F (190°C) gas mark 5.

PERSIAN PILAF

A recipe that depends for its quality on the candied peel. In Persia, this would be sliced thinly from large pieces. These are available but they are not always easy to find so you may have to buy ready-chopped mixed peel.

2 tablespoons olive oil
3-4 lb (1.5-1.75 kg) roasting chicken, jointed (see page 13)
¼ pint (150 ml) chicken stock (see page 22)
5-6 saffron strands
1 ounce (25 g) butter
3 medium carrots, chopped
1 medium onion, thinly sliced
3 ounces (75 g) flaked almonds
4 ounces (100 g) candied peel, thinly sliced or chopped, and rinsed if necessary

salt and black pepper
For the rice
2 tablespoons oil
12 ounces (350 g) long-grain rice
1 ounce (25 g) seedless raisins
1 ounce (25 g) flaked almonds
¼ teaspoon cinnamon or 1 stick crumbled

Preparation 20 minutes
Cooking 1 hour

MENU PLANNING: Serve with broccoli or cauliflower. Drink cider or lager.

1. Heat the oil in a heavy-based saucepan, add the chicken and cook until evenly browned.
2. Add the stock and saffron, cover and simmer for 30 minutes.
3. Heat the butter in another pan, add the carrots and onion and cook gently for about 10 minutes.
4. Stir in the almonds and candied peel, then stir into the chicken.
5. Season with salt and pepper and simmer until tender – about 10 minutes.
6. For the rice, heat the oil in a large saucepan and

fry the rice until it becomes semi-translucent. Stir in 1½ times its volume of water, the raisins, almonds and cinnamon, cover and simmer until all the water is absorbed and the rice is just tender — about 12-14 minutes.

7. Serve on a large warmed dish with the chicken and its sauce in the centre surrounded by the rice.

BLANQUETTE DE POULET

Veal and rabbit are normally used for blanquettes, but chicken is just as suitable. Cut the bird into more pieces than you normally would; the breast into 5, the thighs and the drumsticks, if large enough, into 2, by cutting across the bone. Keep the back and wings for another dish – a paella perhaps (see page 89).

2 pints (1.2 litres) stock
  (see page 22) or water
3½-4 lb (1.5-1.75 kg)
  chicken, skinned and
  jointed (see page 13)
12 small onions
6 cloves
1 carrot, chopped
2 bay leaves
2 teaspoons fresh thyme or
  1 teaspoon dried thyme
salt and white pepper

4 ounces (100 g) button
  mushrooms
1¼ ounces (40 g) butter
2 tablespoons flour
¼ pint (150 ml) thick cream
2 eggs yolks
4 teaspoons lemon juice
For garnish
chopped fresh parsley

Preparation 15 minutes
Cooking 1 hour 15 minutes

MENU PLANNING: Serve with new potatoes and buttered carrots. Drink a full-bodied white wine, say a Burgundy or Rhône.

1. Bring the stock or water to the boil, add the chicken and bring back to the boil.
2. Add the onions, one stuck with the cloves, the carrot, bay leaves, thyme, salt and pepper and simmer, covered, until the chicken is almost tender – about 30 minutes.
3. Add the mushrooms and simmer for 5 minutes.
4. Transfer the chicken and vegetables to a warm serving dish and keep warm.
5. Blend the butter and flour together until smooth then gradually blend in ¾ pint (450 ml) strained stock. Return to the pan and bring to the boil, stirring, then simmer gently for 20 minutes.*
6. Blend the cream and egg yolks together then gradually stir in 5 tablespoons of the sauce.
7. Stir the egg yolk mixture into the sauce and cook over a low heat, stirring constantly, until the sauce thickens. Do not allow it to boil. Stir in the lemon juice.
8. Pour the sauce over the chicken and vegetables and sprinkle with parsley.

KAJU MURGH KARI

Although this is quite a hot curry it is not overpowering and the exciting tastes aren't lost. For a good curry it is essential to fry the onions and garlic gently and slowly. When cooked it should be thick and on the dry side.

3 tablespoons oil
2 large onions, chopped
3 cloves of garlic, crushed
1½ teaspoons fresh ginger, finely grated
3 tablespoons curry powder
1 teaspoon chilli powder
3 ripe tomatoes, peeled and chopped
2 tablespoons chopped fresh coriander or mint leaves
salt

3-4 lb (1.5-1.75 kg) roasting chicken, jointed (see page 13)
2 teaspoons garam masala
3 fluid ounces (75 ml) plain yoghurt
4 ounces (100 g) cashew nuts, finely chopped or ground

Preparation 15 minutes
Cooking 1 hour 20 minutes

MENU PLANNING: Serve with rice, chapatis, cucumber, yoghurt and pickles.
Drink lager.

1. Heat the oil in a large saucepan, add the onion, garlic and ginger and gently fry, stirring occasionally, until golden and soft.
2. Add the curry powder and chilli powder and stir for 1 minute.
3. Add the tomatoes, herbs and salt and cook until reduced to a pulp.
4. Add the chicken pieces and stir well to coat them thoroughly in the spicy mixture. Cover tightly and simmer gently until tender – about 45 minutes.
5. Stir in the garam masala then gradually add the yoghurt, stirring well after each addition. Simmer, uncovered, for 5 minutes.
6. Stir in the cashew nuts and heat through.

CHICKEN IN ALMOND SAUCE

A Spanish recipe which we do with a roasting chicken.

chicken giblets
3½-4 lb (1.5-1.75 kg)
  roasting chicken, jointed
  (see page 13)
2 ounces (50 g) butter
2 tablespoons olive oil
2 medium onions, chopped
5 cloves of garlic, chopped
1 tablespoon chopped fresh
  parsley or 1½ teaspoons
  dried parsley
4 ounces (100 g) ground
  almonds

¼ pint (150 ml) dry white
  wine
salt and black pepper
1 egg yolk

Preparation 15 minutes
Stock 30 minutes
Cooking 1 hour 30 minutes
Temperature 350°F
  (180°C) gas mark 4 for
  1 hour

MENU PLANNING: Serve with rice and stir-fried cabbage.
Drink a dry white Spanish wine, say a white Rioja or Valdepeñas.

1. Simmer giblets in ½ pint (300 ml) water in a covered saucepan for 20 minutes
2. Heat the butter and oil in a frying pan, add the onions and garlic and fry until soft. Transfer to an oven-proof casserole with a slotted spoon.
3. Fry the chicken in the frying pan until evenly browned, then transfer to the casserole and add the parsley.
4. Strain the stock and stir on to the ground almonds; pour into the pan with the wine, stir well to dislodge the sediment then pour into the casserole.
5. Add the seasoning. Cover and cook for 1 hour at 350°F (180°C) gas mark 4.*
6. Transfer the chicken to a warmed plate. Keep warm.
7. Blend a little of the liquid from the casserole with the egg yolk to make a thin 'cream'. Pour back into the casserole, stirring. Place over a low heat and cook, stirring constantly, until the sauce thickens, but do not allow it to boil. Pour over the chicken.

CHICKEN PAPRIKA

Our version of this well-known Hungarian dish comes from our Hungarian friend, Edith Corfield. Every Hungarian, she says, has their own recipe. Some English and American versions use flour to thicken the sauce, but apart from flouring the chicken pieces, it should be rigorously avoided.

3 tablespoons oil
2 medium onions, finely chopped
1 heaped teaspoon paprika pepper
½ teaspoon cayenne pepper
1 clove of garlic, crushed
1 tomato, peeled and chopped
1 teaspoon tomato purée
1 green pepper, chopped
black pepper
2 ounces (50 g) flour

salt
breast, thighs and drumsticks of a 3½-4 lb (1.5-1.75 kg) roasting chicken
¾ pint (450 ml) chicken stock (see page 22)
1 tablespoon soured cream

Preparation 15 minutes
Cooking 1 hour

MENU PLANNING: Serve
with boiled potatoes and
broccoli.
Drink a Riesling or Pinot
Blanc.

1. Heat half the oil in a large, heavy-based saucepan, add the onions and fry until golden brown.
2. Remove from the heat and stir in the paprika, cayenne, garlic, tomato, tomato purée, green pepper and black pepper.
3. Season the flour with salt then coat the chicken well. Heat the remaining oil in a large frying pan, add the chicken and cook over a moderately high heat until an even light brown.
4. Add the chicken to the vegetables and pour in sufficient stock to just cover. Cover and simmer until tender – about 40 minutes.*
5. Transfer the chicken to a warmed serving dish and keep warm.
6. Boil the sauce to reduce it if necessary then stir in the soured cream.

POLLO AL LATTE

Here is our version of this succulent Italian dish. Do not use more milk than we suggest, otherwise it will take an age to reduce the sauce to a proper thickness. Other meats, such as pork, lamb and kid, can be cooked by the same method.

chicken's liver and skin
4 ounces (100 g) streaky
  bacon, diced
3½-4 lb (1.5-1.75 kg)
  roasting chicken, skinned
  and jointed (see page 13)
1 onion, chopped
¾ pint (450 ml) milk

3 cloves of garlic, chopped
1 teaspoon fennel seeds or
  dill seeds
salt

Preparation 15 minutes
Cooking 1 hour 20 minutes

MENU PLANNING: Serve with steamed potatoes and courgettes tossed in butter. Drink a dry white Italian wine.

1. Finely chop the chicken liver. Chop the chicken skin.
2. In a large, heavy-based saucepan, fry the skin and bacon in their own fat for 2-3 minutes.
3. Add the chicken and fry until lightly browned on one side.
4. Add the onion, turn the chicken over and fry on the other side until lightly browned.
5. Add the milk and simmer for 25 minutes.
6. Add the garlic and fennel or dill seeds, turn the chicken over and simmer for another 25 minutes.
7. Remove the chicken and keep warm.
8. Add the chicken liver to the milk and simmer for 15 minutes, or until reduced to a thick sauce, stirring frequently to free all the delicious cooking crust.
9. Taste for seasoning then pour over the chicken.

CELESTIAL CHICKEN

An earthenware chicken brick is best for this dish because it conforms fairly closely to the chicken's shape. The stuffing liquefies during the cooking and can be spooned out or poured into a jug to make the sauce.

8 ounces (225 g) cream or
  curd cheese
1 teaspoon fennel seeds or
  1½ tablespoons chopped
  fennel leaves
3-4 lb (1.25-1.75 kg)
  roasting chicken
salt and black pepper
¼ pint (150 ml) dry white
  wine

2 tablespoons oil
4 leeks, chopped
4 carrots, chopped
4 sticks of celery, chopped
2 tablespoons brandy

Preparation 15 minutes
Cooking 1 hour 20 minutes
Temperature 400°F
  (200°C) gas mark 6 then
  375°F (190°C) gas mark 5

MENU PLANNING: Serve
with noodles.
Drink a dry white wine.

1. Mix the cheese and fennel together, put inside the chicken and sew up the cavity opening.
2. Put the chicken in the bottom half of a chicken brick, sprinkle with salt and pepper and cook, uncovered, for 20 minutes at 400°F (200°C) gas mark 6.
3. Mix the wine with the oil and pour over the chicken. Surround the bird with the vegetables, cover and cook for 1 hour at 375°F (190°C) gas mark 5.
4. Remove the lid. Heat the brandy in a ladle or large spoon over a naked flame until it ignites then pour, still flaming, on to the chicken. Serve from the brick.

MANDARIN VELVET

A delicate and comparatively simple Chinese dish. The large amount of cornflour produces a slightly gelatinous effect. Other vegetables, for example bean shoots, can be substituted for the peas and mushrooms.

6 tablespoons cornflour
2 egg whites, lightly
  whisked
3½-4 lb (1.5-1.75 kg)
  roasting chicken,
  skinned, flesh cut into ¾
  inch (4 cm) pieces
1 lb (450 g) prepared fresh
  or frozen peas

4 ounces (150 g)
  mushrooms
2 tablespoons soy sauce
salt and black pepper

Preparation 30 minutes
Cooking 40 minutes

MENU PLANNING: Serve with rice and sautéed mixed vegetables: courgettes, broccoli, bamboo shoots and carrots.
Drink rice wine.

1. Mix 3 tablespoons of cornflour with the egg whites and 2 fluid ounces (50 ml) cold water.
2. Add the chicken and leave for 15 minutes.
3. Bring a large saucepan filled with water to the boil. Add a few chicken pieces at a time and simmer for 3 minutes.
4. Remove the chicken with a slotted spoon and rinse in cold water. Continue in this way until all the chicken has been cooked, making sure the water is boiling all the time.
5. Cook the peas and mushrooms in ½ pint (300 ml) simmering water for 2 minutes.
6. Add the chicken, cover, and simmer for 8-10 minutes.
7. Mix the remaining cornflour with any remaining cornflour/egg white/water mixture, or if there is not enough, with a little cold water, then blend with the chicken and vegetables and continue to cook, stirring until the sauce thickens.
8. Stir in the soy sauce and taste for seasoning.

PIPERADE WITH CHICKEN LIVERS

Chicken livers are an interesting addition to this well-known Basque recipe.

2 tablespoons olive oil
2 lb (1 kg) green peppers, sliced fairly thickly
2 lb (1 kg) tomatoes, peeled, quartered and seeds and juice discarded
½ ounce (15 g) butter

1 lb (450 g) chicken livers, chopped
6 eggs
salt and black pepper

Preparation 15 minutes
Cooking 25 minutes

MENU PLANNING: Serve as a supper dish with hot buttered toast.
Drink a red *vin ordinaire*.

1. In a large heavy pan heat the olive oil and gently cook the peppers until soft – about 15 minutes.
2. Add the tomato flesh and heat until it softens.
3. Meanwhile, heat the butter in another pan and cook the livers for 5 minutes stirring occasionally – they should remain pink inside.
4. Beat the eggs, season generously and add to the peppers and tomatoes. Cook, stirring gently, until the mixture resembles soft scrambled eggs – it should not harden or the dish is spoiled.
5. Stir in the livers and serve at once.

POLLO EN SALSA DE HUEVOS

We recommend making the sauce in a double saucepan or in a bowl over a pan of hot water, because it is likely to curdle if heated too fiercely.

3½-4 lb (1.5-1.75 kg) roasting chicken, skinned and jointed (see page 13)
2 ounces (50 g) flour
2 ounces (50 g) butter
2½ fluid ounces (65 ml) white wine
¼ pint (150 ml) chicken stock (see page 22)

salt and black pepper
2 eggs
2 tablespoons lemon juice
1 teaspoon mustard powder
½ teaspoon sugar

Preparation 10 minutes
Cooking 1 hour 10 minutes

MENU PLANNING: Serve with rice and spinach. Drink fruity Spanish white wine, say from Navarra.

1. Coat the chicken in flour. Heat the butter in a large saucepan and cook the chicken until evenly browned.
2. Stir in the wine, stock, salt and pepper, cover, turn down the heat and cook until tender – about 45 minutes.
3. Beat the eggs, lemon juice, mustard and sugar together and heat in a double saucepan or a bowl over a pan of hot water until they thicken, stirring constantly.
4. Stir in some of the juices from the chicken, then pour back on to the chicken and cook very gently, stirring, until the chicken is coated and the liquid almost, but not quite, comes to simmering point.

GALLINA EN PEBRE

This rich and succulent Spanish dish reverses the usual order and first roasts then simmers the bird. To make it less rich, leave out the butter from the simmering liquid.

salt
3½-4 lb (1.5-1.75 kg) roasting chicken
chicken's liver or 2 ounces (50 g) chicken livers

1 teaspoon dried thyme or 2 teaspoons chopped fresh thyme
4 cloves of garlic
3 ounces (75 g) butter

1 tablespoon olive oil
1 tablespoon lemon juice
¼ pint (150 ml) stock (see page 22)
¼ pint (150 ml) dry white wine
1 tablespoon chopped fresh parsley or a heaped

teaspoon of dried parsley
2 bay leaves
1 egg yolk, beaten

Preparation 5 minutes
Cooking 1 hour 25 minutes
Temperature 400°F (200°C) gas mark 6

MENU PLANNING: Serve with boiled rice and a green salad.
Drink a good red Rioja.

1. Sprinkle salt inside the chicken then put the chicken liver and the thyme into the cavity.

2. Grind the garlic, half the butter, the oil, lemon juice and 1 teaspoon salt together then spread over the chicken.

3. Roast for 30 minutes at 400°F (200°C) gas mark 6, basting twice. The coating may char, but this does not matter.

4. Put the stock, wine, parsley, bay leaves and remaining butter into a large saucepan, add the chicken and cooking juices, cover and simmer for 45 minutes.

5. Transfer to a warmed serving dish and keep warm.

6. Strain the simmering liquor and gradually blend a little with the egg yolk to make a thin 'cream'. Stir this back into the liquor and cook over a low heat, stirring constantly, until it thickens to make a sauce to serve with the chicken.

VALLÉE D'AUGE

This gloriously rich but quite simple dish is not for tender stomachs. We give it at its richest, but the wary or frail can reduce the butter and use thin cream.

2 ounces (50 g) butter
3½-4 lb (1.5-1.75 kg)
  roasting chicken, jointed
  (see page 13)
3 tablespoons calvados
1 medium onion, diced
1 tablespoon fresh chopped
  parsley or 1 teaspoon
  dried parsley

sprig of fresh thyme or ¼
  teaspoon dried thyme
salt and black pepper
6 tablespoons cider
6 tablespoons thick cream

Preparation 10 minutes
Cooking 1 hour 10 minutes

MENU PLANNING: Serve with plain boiled potatoes and boiled onions. Drink cider.

1. Heat the butter in a heavy-based saucepan, add the chicken and cook until evenly browned.
2. Heat the calvados in a ladle over a naked flame until it ignites then pour over the chicken. Don't be alarmed by the flame the spirit will produce.
3. Add the onion, parsley, thyme, salt, pepper and cider, cover and simmer until tender – about 45 minutes.
4. Transfer the chicken to a warm serving dish.
5. Stir the cream into the pan and heat gently. When it just starts to bubble pour over the chicken.

POLLO PISTO

For the best results use a fresh chicken. The chicken's own liver will be sufficient for the sauce, but today when shop chickens are liable to come with none (and two hearts or gizzards in compensation) you may have to add 2 ounces (50 g) chicken livers.

3½-4 lb (1.5-1.75 kg) roasting chicken, cut in half lengthways
1 ounce (25 g) butter
salt and pepper
1 tablespoon olive oil
juice of ½ a lemon
For the sauce
2 slices of streaky bacon, diced
1 small onion, minced
2-3 large mushrooms, chopped

½ teaspoon flour
2 tablespoons Marsala, sweet Madeira or sherry
1 teaspoon brown sugar
¼ teaspoon ground nutmeg
salt
chicken's liver, or 2 ounces (50 g) chicken livers, minced

Preparation 10 minutes
Cooking 50 minutes

MENU PLANNING: Serve with rice and buttered leeks. Drink a red country wine.

1. Beat the chicken halves flat with a wooden mallet – the bones will break, but this does not matter.
2. Lightly butter a very large heavy pan (or 2 small ones) and add the chicken halves, cut side down.
3. Melt the remaining butter and pour over the chicken, season with salt and pepper, then cover each half with a weighted saucepan lid and cook over a low heat for 35 minutes.
4. Turn the halves, sprinkle with olive oil and lemon juice and cook in the same way for 10 minutes.
5. For the sauce, fry the bacon in a small saucepan for 2 minutes. Add the remaining ingredients, except the liver, cover tightly and cook gently for 25 minutes.
6. Add the liver and simmer for another 5 minutes.
7. Divide the chicken into portions, place on a heated serving dish and pour the sauce over.

CHICKEN CHINOISE

This is a Chinese dish and needs one or two specialised ingredients, so perhaps you'll have to visit your local 'Chinatown', although nowadays many supermarkets have Chinese shelves.

3 oz (75 g) butter
1 small onion, chopped
1 tablespoon oil
3½-4 lb (1.5-1.75 kg)
  roasting chicken, jointed
  (see page 13)
4 tablespoons flour
½ pint (300 ml) chicken
  stock (see page 22)
½ pint (300 ml) dry cider
1 tablespoon yellow bean
  sauce
5 pieces stem ginger, thinly
  sliced

2 tablespoons syrup from
  the stem ginger jar
8 ounce (225 g) can water
  chestnuts, drained
salt

Preparation 15 minutes
Cooking 1½ hours
Temperature 350°F
  (180°C) gas mark 4

MENU PLANNING: Serve
with rice or noodles and
mange tout peas.
Drink rice wine.

1. Heat 1 ounce (25 g) butter in a large saucepan, add the onion and cook until soft. Transfer to an oven-proof casserole with a slotted spoon. Add the oil to the pan.
2. Coat the chicken in 2 tablespoons flour and fry in the pan until golden brown then transfer to the casserole.
3. Melt the remaining butter in the pan, stir in the remaining flour then gradually stir in the chicken stock and cider. Bring to the boil, stirring, and cook until the sauce thickens.
4. Add the yellow bean sauce, ginger and ginger syrup. Pour over the chicken, cover and cook for 1 hour at 350°F (180°C) gas mark 4.
5. Add the water chestnuts, taste for salt and return to the oven for 5 minutes.

ORIENTAL GRILLED WINGS

The spices can be varied according to what you have but the ones we suggest make a successful combination. Putting them all in a blender with the oil and vinegar mixes them thoroughly, but they can equally well just be stirred together.

For the marinade

3 teaspoons ground coriander
2 teaspoons ground cumin
2 teaspoons ground cinnamon
1 teaspoon ground cardamom
½ teaspoon ground cloves
½ teaspoon cayenne pepper
3 tablespoons white wine vinegar

2 tablespoons olive oil
1 tablespoon tomato purée
salt
1 onion, finely chopped

3 lb (1.5 kg) chicken wings, ends removed and the joints cut in half

Preparation 15 minutes
Marinating 4-12 hours
Cooking 10 minutes

MENU PLANNING: Serve with wholemeal bread and bowls of mixed salad. Drink a light red wine.

1. Mix all the ingredients for the marinade together in a blender or stir them together.
2. Pour over the chicken and turn the joints over until they are all thoroughly coated.
3. Leave in a cool place overnight or for at least 4 hours.
4. Cook under a hot grill for 5-7 minutes on each side.

CHICKIE LICKIES

This combination of chicken and cheese is unusually tasty. Chickie Lickies also look intriguing and it can be quite a surprise to cut into one. You can use any cheese, though we like a strong blue one such as Roquefort.

3 ounces (75 g) butter
5 ounces (150 g) Roquefort
* or other blue cheese,*
* grated or crumbled*
2 cloves of garlic, crushed
3½ lb (1.5 kg) roasted
* chicken, flesh removed*
* and minced*
2 eggs

salt and black pepper
2 ounces (50 g) dried
* breadcrumbs*
oil for deep frying

Preparation 30 minutes
Chilling 40 minutes
Cooking 15-20 minutes

MENU PLANNING: Serve on a bed of mashed potatoes with courgettes. Drink a dry white Italian wine such as Frascati.

1. Mash the butter, cheese and garlic together and divide into 12 walnut-sized pieces. Put into the refrigerator for at least 10 minutes to harden.
2. Mix the chicken with the eggs, salt and pepper.
3. Wrap the chicken mixture around the butter and cheese and roll into smooth balls.
4. Coat the chicken balls in breadcrumbs and chill for at least 30 minutes.
5. Heat the oil in a deep-fat frying pan to 375°F (190°C) then fry the balls in batches for 5-7 minutes until golden and crisp. Drain on absorbent paper.

ELABORATE DISHES

WHITE CLOUD

This Chinese roast takes its name from the prawn crackers which are served with it, but even more impressive is the deep chestnut colour of the roast bird itself. The temperature is important. Cooked at more than 350°F (180°C) gas mark 4, the skin may burn.

3½-4 lb (1.5-1.75 kg)
  roasting chicken
salt
3 leeks, cut into 1 inch (2.5
  cm) lengths
3 cloves of garlic, crushed
1½ tablespoons dark soy
  sauce

2 tablespoons dry sherry
1 teaspoon clear honey
For serving
prawn crackers

Preparation 25 minutes
Cooking 2 hours
Temperature 350°F
  (180°C) gas mark 4

MENU PLANNING: Serve with fried rice and shrimps and a Chinese sauté of mixed vegetables.
Drink hot rice wine.

1. Rub the bird with salt.
2. Mix the leeks with the garlic, and 1 teaspoon each of soy sauce and sherry. Place inside the chicken and sew it up.
3. Mix the remaining soy sauce and sherry with the honey and rub into the chicken. Leave for 15 minutes.
4. Put the chicken in a smallish roasting pan or the bottom half of a chicken brick (so that the cooking juices do not burn), pour the sauce over again and roast the chicken for 1¾ hours at 350°F (180°C) gas mark 4. Turn it every 15 minutes, first on to its sides then on to its breast, and baste it.
5. Divide the chicken into joints then reassemble in a chicken-like shape. Serve with the prawn crackers. (These are prepared in a few seconds by frying in medium-hot oil.)

RIJSTAFEL

This great dish from the East Indies, served with numerous side dishes of nuts, fruit, vegetables and pickles, was invented by Dutch settlers. We give the central chicken and rice dish.

3½-4 lb (1.5-1.75 kg)
  roasting chicken
1 lb (450 g) onions (one
  onion should be small)
2 bay leaves
salt and black pepper
3 tablespoons oil
1 lb (450 g) long-grain rice
2 tablespoons peanut
  butter
½ teaspoon chilli powder
4 ounces (100 g) ham,
  diced
1 teaspoon ground cumin

1½ teaspoons ground
  coriander
¼ teaspoon allspice
2 cloves of garlic, crushed
4 ounces (100 g) shelled
  prawns
For the garnish
1 hard-boiled egg, chopped
½ cucumber, chopped
½ sweet red pepper,
  chopped

Preparation 10 minutes
Cooking 2 hours

MENU PLANNING: Serve with bowls of chutneys, pickles, fresh tomatoes, cashew nuts, chopped bananas, grated coconut and raisins.
Drink lager.

1. Place the chicken, the small onion, the bay leaves and salt and pepper in a large saucepan, add water to almost cover, bring to the boil and simmer gently until the chicken is tender – about 1¼ hours.
2. Remove the chicken and leave to cool slightly.
3. Heat half the oil in another pan, add the rice and cook until semi-transparent.
4. Stir in 28 fluid ounces (700 ml) of the stock in which the chicken was cooked, bring to the boil, cover and simmer until the liquid is absorbed and the rice is tender – about 12-14 minutes.
5. Finely chop the remaining onions and fry gently in a large frying pan in the remaining oil until they start to colour.
6. Stir in the peanut butter and chilli powder.
7. Skin the chicken, and chop the flesh fairly finely.
8. Stir into the onions with the ham and rice and continue to heat until it starts to catch.
9. Stir in the spices, garlic and prawns.
10. Transfer to a warmed serving dish and garnish with the hard-boiled egg, cucumber and red pepper.

MEXICAN CHOWDER

This Mexican dish may sound a mush, but is in fact delicious, the corn and chicken complementing the strong vegetable and olive flavours.

1 ounce (25 g) butter
3½-4 lb (1.5-1.75 kg)
  roasting chicken, jointed
  (see page 13)
¾ pint (450 ml) chicken
  stock or water
2 cloves of garlic, crushed
salt
2 medium onions, chopped
2 green peppers, chopped
14 ounce (400 g) can of
  tomatoes, drained

2 fresh tomatoes, peeled
  and chopped
4 ounces (100 g) stoned
  black olives
2 tablespoons flour
1½ lb (750 g) canned
  sweetcorn kernels,
  drained
4 rashers of streaky bacon

Preparation 25 minutes
Cooking 1 hour 15 minutes
Temperature 400°F
  (200°C) gas mark 6

MENU PLANNING: Serve
with rice and okra.
Drink lager or a white
Californian wine.

1. Heat the butter in a heavy pan, add the chicken and fry until evenly browned.
2. Transfer to an oven-proof casserole, add the stock, or water, garlic and salt and simmer, covered, until the chicken is tender – about 30 minutes. Remove the chicken flesh from the bones.
3. Meanwhile, fry the onions and peppers in the heavy pan over a moderate heat until they soften, then add the canned and fresh tomatoes and olives and cook for 5 minutes.
4. Stir in the flour, then gradually stir in about 8 fluid ounces (225 ml) of the stock in which the chicken was simmered. Bring to the boil, stirring, then simmer for 2 minutes.
5. Place alternate layers of sweetcorn, chicken meat and vegetable sauce in an oven-proof casserole, beginning and ending with sweetcorn.
6. Top with the bacon and bake for 20 minutes at 400°F (200°C) gas mark 6 then place under a hot grill for a few moments to crisp the bacon.

GOURMET HONGROISE

This Hungarian dish depends on the sauce (the chicken fillets and meatballs are bland in flavour).

For the sauce
1 ounce (25 g) butter
1 onion, chopped
the chicken's bones
½ teaspoon paprika pepper
¼ teaspoon cayenne pepper
black pepper
8 ounces (225 ml) thick
  cream

For the meatballs
8 ounces (225 g) minced
  chicken (from back and
  wings)
8 ounces (225 g) minced
  veal
1 small onion, chopped
flour

For the lesco
½ ounce (15 g) butter
1 large onion, chopped
2 green peppers, chopped
4 tomatoes, peeled and
  chopped
salt

salt
6 fillets (see page 15) from
  a 5 lb (2.25 kg) chicken
2 cloves of garlic, crushed
2 ounces (50 g) butter

Preparation 35 minutes
Cooking 1 hour 50 minutes

MENU PLANNING: Serve with boiled noodles and courgettes.
Drink a Hungarian Riesling.

1. For the sauce, heat the butter or chicken fat in a heavy saucepan, add the onion and cook until soft. Add the bones and seasonings, cover with water, cover and simmer for 1 hour. Strain then boil until reduced to ½ pint (300 ml). Stir in the cream and reheat but do not boil.
2. For the meatballs, mix the chicken, veal and onion and form into 6 balls, using a little flour to make them easier to handle. Place in a covered steamer or colander over boiling water for 30 minutes.
3. For the lesco heat the butter, add the onion and cook until soft then stir in the remaining ingredients and 1 tablespoon water. Cover and simmer until tender – about 30 minutes.
4. Sprinkle salt over the fillets and rub in the garlic. Heat the butter in a frying pan, add the chicken and cook for about 15 minutes, turning the fillets halfway through.
5. Place a fillet and a meatball side by side on each plate. Pour the sauce on then top with lesco.

CHICKEN AND WATERCRESS

This is excellent both hot and cold. For the latter put the chicken pieces on to a bed of salad and pour the sauce into the centre like a dip.

3½-4 lb (1.5-1.75 kg)
  roasting chicken
1 onion, halved
1 carrot, halved
1 leek, halved
1 stick of celery, halved
2 cloves
1 bay leaf
3 fresh parsley stalks or
  1 teaspoon dried parsley
1 sprig fresh thyme or
  ¼ teaspoon dried thyme
8 black peppercorns,
½ tablespoon sea salt

For the sauce
1 ounce (25 g) butter
1½ teaspoons flour
½ pint (300 ml) chicken
  stock (from cooking the
  bird)
2 ounces (50 g) watercress
  leaves, finely chopped
¼ pint (150 ml) thick cream
2 teaspoons Dijon mustard
2 teaspoons lemon juice
salt and black pepper

Preparation 10 minutes
Cooking 1½ hours

MENU PLANNING: Serve with new potatoes and mixed sautéed carrots and courgettes.
Drink a Sancerre or Pouilly Fumé.

1. Put the chicken in a flame-proof casserole and surround it with the vegetables, cloves, herbs and peppercorns. Sprinkle on the salt and pour in enough hot water to come halfway up the legs. Bring just to the boil quickly, removing any scum that rises. Cover and simmer very gently for 1-1¼ hours until the flesh is tender. Check to make sure that the water is not boiling too hard or the chicken will be tough.
2. Transfer the chicken to a warmed dish, cover and keep warm.
3. Strain the liquid, measure ½ pint (300 ml) and reheat.
4. For the sauce, melt the butter in a saucepan, stir in the flour and cook for 1 minute then gradually stir in the stock. Bring to the boil, stirring, then simmer for 2 minutes. Cool slightly.
5. Blend the watercress with the cream.
6. Stir the watercress and cream, mustard and lemon juice into the sauce and reheat, stirring – do not boil. Taste for seasoning then pour over the chicken.

PAELLA

A paella can include any number of different meat and fish ingredients. The proportion of these to the rice can also vary. In Spain, if the dish is treated as a preliminary one, like pasta in Italy, it often consists of little except rice. But if it is to be a main course use at least the quantities we suggest. As for saffron, we give the amount usually recommended, but, heretical as it may sound, suggest adding a drop or two of yellow colouring as well. Don't use turmeric as it has an inappropriate flavour of its own. The quantities given below will feed at least ten.

3 tablespoons olive oil
2 medium onions, chopped
4 cloves of garlic, finely chopped
2 red peppers, chopped
4 tomatoes, sliced
2 lb (750 g) poussin, jointed, or 6 chicken wing joints
2 ounces (50 g) hot chorizo, or other spicy, dry sausage, sliced

2¼ lb (1.2 kg) short-grain rice
10 saffron strands, soaked in a little milk
4 ounces (100 g) dried peas
12 mussels in their shells
8 ounces (225 g) other shellfish
salt and black pepper
10 large unshelled prawns

Preparation 10 minutes
Cooking 1 hour

MENU PLANNING: Needs no vegetables.
Drink a Spanish white wine.

1. Heat the oil in a large pan, add the onions, garlic and half the peppers and fry until softened.
2. Add the tomatoes and continue to cook for 3-4 minutes, stirring occasionally.
3. Add the poussin or wings and chorizo and fry until evenly browned, turning once or twice.
4. Add the rice and cook, stirring, until translucent.
5. Stir in 1½ times the rice's volume of water, and the saffron, peas and remaining peppers. Simmer, uncovered, for 15 minutes.
6. Add the mussels and shellfish, stir again and taste for seasoning. Place the prawns on top and cover till all is thoroughly heated before serving.

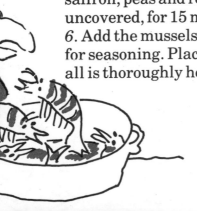

89

POULE AU POT HENRI IV

This economical and delicious French dish was named after the 16th-century king who wanted all his subjects to have a fowl in the pot every Sunday. Untraditionally, we use a roaster.

4½ lb (2 kg) roasting chicken

For the court bouillon
giblets (except the liver) and the wing tips of the chicken
small knuckle of veal or piece of bacon
2 carrots, roughly chopped
2 small turnips, roughly chopped
2 onions, one of them stuck with 4 cloves
2 leeks, roughly chopped
1 stick of celery, roughly chopped
1 bay leaf
sprig of fresh parsley
salt and black pepper

For the stuffing
5 slices stale white bread, crusts removed, soaked in ¼ pint (150 ml) milk
the chicken's liver
1 thick slice of ham or bacon, chopped
pinch of nutmeg
2 cloves of garlic, chopped
2 tablespoons chopped fresh parsley
salt and black pepper
2 eggs, beaten

Preparation 25 minutes
Cooking 2 hours 30 minutes
Cooling 2 hours

MENU PLANNING: Serve with buttered baked parsnips or turnips and cabbage. Drink a French country wine, say from Provence.

1. For the court bouillon, simmer all the ingredients for 1 hour in 4 pints (2.25 litres) water in a large, covered saucepan, removing scum as it forms. Allow to cool and remove the fat.
2. For the stuffing, mash the bread and milk and add the remaining ingredients, mixing in the eggs last.
3. Place the stuffing in the bird's cavity and under the flap of neck skin. Wrap the bird in a clean cloth tying it securely.
4. Strain the court bouillon and bring to the boil in a large, heavy pan. Lower in the chicken and simmer, covered, for 1½ hours. Do not overcook.
5. Remove from the stock. Serve the stock as a sauce.

POLISH RISSOLES

These rissoles are messy to prepare as the beaten egg whites make the mixture hard to handle, but that is why they are so light. You will need a hot oven ready to cook them in when they have been fried.

For the sauce
3 hard-boiled egg yolks, sieved
2 teaspoons lemon juice
1 teaspoon sugar
4 teaspoons mustard
¼ pint (150 ml) strong stock
3 teaspoons capers, or chopped gherkins
For the rissoles
3 ounces (75 g) butter
2 ounces (50 g) mushrooms, chopped
3 eggs, 2 separated

2 slices of bread, crusts removed, soaked in milk
2 chicken breasts, skinned and minced
salt and black pepper
2 ounces (50 g) dried breadcrumbs

Sauce 15 minutes
Preparation 30 minutes
Chilling 30 minutes
Cooking 30 minutes
Temperature 400°F (200°C) gas mark 6

MENU PLANNING: Serve with spicy red cabbage cooked with caraway seeds, brown sugar and vinegar.
Drink a German white wine.

1. For the sauce, cream the egg yolks with the lemon juice, sugar and mustard then gradually blend in the stock. Add the capers, cover and chill well.
2. For the rissoles, heat ½ ounce (15 g) butter in a frying pan, add the mushrooms and cook slowly until softened.
3. Cream the 2 egg yolks with ½ ounce (15 g) butter.
4. Squeeze the soaked bread, mash it then add to the egg yolk and butter mixture with the chicken and salt and pepper.
5. Whisk the 2 egg whites until stiff then fold into the mixture with the mushrooms. Form into small balls and leave in the refrigerator for at least 30 minutes.
6. Mix the remaining egg with the breadcrumbs and use to coat the chicken balls.
7. Heat the remaining butter in a frying pan to a fairly high temperature, but do not let it burn. Fry the chicken balls until golden brown all over then arrange them on a baking tray and put them in an oven at 400°F (200°C) gas mark 6 for 10 minutes.
10. Serve the rissoles and sauce separately.

GRILLED CHICKEN MAINTENON

Louis XIV's chef named this dish after the king's mistress, the Marquise de Maintenon. For a really splendid result, use slices of home-made wholemeal bread for the toast. Because each serving sits on a slice of toast, the chicken must be jointed to make the right number of servings. For six people a good division is: 2 breasts, 2 thighs and 2 servings made up of a wing and a drumstick each. Alternatively, use 3 poussins, divided in half.

4 ounces (100 g) butter
juice of ½ a lemon
3-4 lb (1.5-1.75 kg) chicken, jointed (see page 13)
4 ounces (100 g) mushrooms, sliced
4 ounces (100 g) cooked tongue, chopped
2 chicken livers, chopped
6 fluid ounces (175 ml) dry white wine or dry sherry

2 sprigs of fresh thyme or 1 teaspoon dried thyme
salt and black pepper
6 slices of bread for toast
For the garnish
sprigs of parsley

Preparation 20 minutes
Cooking 35 minutes

MENU PLANNING: Serve with buttered French beans and braised celery. Drink a fine claret.

1. Melt 2 ounces (50 g) butter and mix with the lemon juice.
2. Grill the chicken, basting occasionally with the butter/lemon juice mixture.
3. Gently cook the mushrooms and tongue together in a frying pan in 1 ounce (25 g) butter for 3-4 minutes, stirring occasionally.
4. Cook the chicken livers very lightly in the final ounce (25 g) of butter in a frying pan, then chop them finely and set aside to keep warm. Drain the cooking juices and reserve.
5. Bring the wine to the boil in a small, covered saucepan then add the livers, thyme, salt, pepper and the cooking juices from the tongue and mushrooms and heat through gently.
6. Toast the bread.
7. Assemble each serving in the following order: toast at the bottom (buttered if you like), a layer of the tongue and mushroom mixture, a joint of chicken then the liver and wine sauce. Garnish with parsley.

CHICKEN KIEV

This spectacular Russian dish is also well known in Italy – as *'pollo sorpresa'*. Make sure the chicken is sewn up tightly around its 'surprise' butter filling and that each piece is dipped twice in the coating. Warn guests that the liquid butter may spurt from the chicken when it is cut and that it will be hot.

4 ounces (100 g) butter
2 tablespoons chopped
  parsley
1 tablespoon grated lemon
  rind
1 tablespoon lemon juice
2 cloves of garlic, crushed
salt and black pepper

6 chicken breasts, skinned
  and boned (see page 14)
2 eggs, beaten
6 ounces (175 g) fresh
  white breadcrumbs
oil for deep frying.

Preparation 1 hour
Chilling 30 minutes
Cooking 6 minutes

MENU PLANNING: Serve with creamed potatoes and a lettuce and avocado salad. Drink a dry white wine from the Loire.

1. Cream the butter with the parsley, lemon rind and juice, garlic and seasoning. Shape into a block and leave in the refrigerator or freezer to harden.
2. Beat the chicken breasts flat. It is easier to do this between sheets of greaseproof paper.
3. Cut the butter into 6 long thin 'fingers' and wrap each in a chicken breast. Sew up tightly with needle and thread.
4. Dip each breast in egg then coat well with breadcrumbs. Repeat once more.
5. Heat the oil to about 375°F (190°C) in a deep-fat frying pan and fry the chicken until golden brown. This will take 5-6 minutes. Drain on absorbent paper.
6. Remove the threads before serving.

SAUTÉ AUX OLIVES

This dish has the rich aroma and flavour that is so typical of the cooking of the south of France. Use fresh herbs if possible. Thyme and marjoram can be picked in winter, but have less flavour, so it is really a summer recipe. The dry black olives from France and Morocco are easily stoned and have the strong taste that this dish needs.

3 cloves of garlic
6 sprigs of fresh thyme and
  1 sprig each of thyme,
  marjoram and basil
4 lb (1.75 kg) roasting
  chicken, jointed (see page
  13)
juice of ½ a lemon
3 tablespoons olive oil

4 fluid ounces (100 ml) red
  or dry white wine
2 anchovy fillets
4 tomatoes, chopped
4 ounces (100 g) black
  olives, stoned

Preparation 30 minutes
Cooking 1 hour

MENU PLANNING: Serve with baked potatoes and buttered peas.
Drink a dry Provençal rosé.

1. Thinly slice 1 clove of garlic and insert a slice with a small sprig of thyme between the skin and flesh of each joint then sprinkle the joints with lemon juice.
2. Heat the oil in a frying pan and fry the joints, skin side first, until evenly browned, turning once or twice.
3. Cover and cook for 20 minutes then transfer with most of the oil to an oven-proof casserole. Cover and place in an oven at the lowest temperature at which it will function efficiently while finishing the dish.
4. Stir the wine into the oil remaining in the pan and boil until slightly syrupy.
5. Crush the anchovies with the remaining garlic and stir into the wine with a sprig each of thyme, marjoram and basil and the tomatoes.
6. Simmer until the tomatoes are soft, then add the olives.
7. Place the chicken on a warmed serving dish and pour the sauce over.

CHICKEN PROVENÇAL

For this we use a classic rich sauce from the south of France. The result bears some resemblance to Chicken Marengo (see page 50) but is cooked on top of, not in, the oven, includes onions and uses red instead of white wine.

1 tablespoon olive oil
1 ounce (25 g) butter
3 medium onions, chopped
3 medium carrots, chopped
1 stick of celery, chopped
2 slices of streaky bacon, chopped
3 cloves of garlic, finely chopped
14 ounce (400 g) can of tomatoes
1 heaped teaspoonful sugar
1 tablespoon white wine vinegar

¼ pint (150 ml) red wine
salt and black pepper
1 tablespoon chopped fresh basil and parsley
3 tablespoons oil
3½-4 lb (1.5-1.75 kg) roasting chicken
2 ounces (50 g) flour
8 ounces (225 g) button mushrooms

Preparation 10 minutes
Cooking 1 hour 15 minutes

MENU PLANNING: Serve with new potatoes and spinach.
Drink a red Rhône.

1. Heat the oil and butter in a flame-proof casserole, add the onions, carrots, celery, bacon and garlic, cover and cook over a moderate heat for 10 minutes.
2. Remove the lid and heat more strongly until the vegetables start to brown.
3. Add the tomatoes, sugar, vinegar, wine, salt, pepper and herbs and simmer for 15 minutes.
4. Meanwhile, heat the oil in a frying pan and coat the chicken in flour then fry the chicken in the oil until evenly browned.
5. Add the chicken to the vegetables, cover and simmer for 40 minutes.
6. Add the mushrooms and simmer for 5 minutes.

SENEGAL CHICKEN

When we discovered this recipe it opened up a new culinary world to us – cooking with fresh coconut.

12 black peppercorns, or
  1 teaspoon ground black
  pepper
4 cloves, or ½ teaspoon
  ground cloves
½ teaspoon ground ginger
salt
3½-4 lb (1.5-1.75 kg)
  roasting chicken, jointed
  (see page 13)

4 tablespoons oil
3 medium onions, finely
  chopped
1 coconut
1 ounce (25 g) butter
1 teaspoon cayenne pepper

Preparation 25 minutes
Cooking 1 hour

MENU PLANNING: Serve with boiled millet or cracked wheat and grilled tomatoes. Drink a dry red Algerian wine.

1. Grind the peppercorns and cloves, if necessary, and mix with the ginger and salt. Coat the chicken pieces with this mixture.
2. Heat the oil in a large frying pan, add the onions and cook gently until soft.
3. Add the chicken and cook over a low heat, turning frequently, for 40 minutes. Transfer the chicken to a warmed serving dish and keep warm.
4. Meanwhile, crack the coconut, reserve the 'milk' (about ¼ pint/150 ml), extract the flesh and grate it.
5. Heat the butter in a saucepan, add the grated coconut and cook, stirring occasionally, for 10-15 minutes, until softened and starting to turn golden.
6. Stir the coconut milk into the onions, bring to the boil and simmer for 5 minutes then season with salt and cayenne pepper.
7. To serve, spoon the coconut over the chicken then pour the coconut milk and onion mixture over.

CHICKEN BÉARNAISE

This classic French recipe uses a boiling fowl. Make the sauce while the chicken is cooking.

For the stuffing
chicken's liver and
  heart
2 ounces (50 g) fresh
  breadcrumbs
4 ounces (100 g) sausage-
  meat
1 egg
1 tablespoon chopped fresh
  parsley or 2 teaspoons
  dried parsley
2 teaspoons dried mixed
  herbs
salt and black pepper
¼ pint (150 ml) milk
butter for frying
4 lb (1.75 kg) boiling fowl
1 onion, roughly chopped
2 carrots, roughly chopped

1 turnip, roughly chopped
1 stick of celery
1 leek, roughly chopped
For the sauce
1 small onion, finely
  chopped
1 teaspoon finely chopped
  chives
1 teaspoon finely chopped
  parsley
3 tablespoons olive oil
1 teaspoon lemon juice
salt and black pepper
1 egg

Preparation 30 minutes
Cooking 3 hours 10
  minutes

MENU PLANNING: Serve
with additional vegetables
that have been added to the
chicken 20 minutes before the
end of the cooking.
Drink a dry red wine, say
from Languedoc.

1. For the stuffing, poach the liver and heart in a little water for 5 minutes, then mince them and mix with the breadcrumbs, sausage-meat, egg, herbs, salt and pepper and add sufficient milk to moisten to a stiff consistency. Stuff the bird and sew it up.
2. Heat the butter in a heavy-based saucepan, add the bird and cook until evenly browned.
3. Just cover with water, add the vegetables, cover and simmer gently for 3 hours.
4. For the sauce, stir the onion, chives and parsley into the olive oil and lemon juice and add salt and pepper.
5. Lightly boil the egg – 3 minutes – then stir the half-cooked yolk and the roughly chopped white into the sauce.
6. Serve the chicken sliced and accompanied by the sauce.

MOROCCAN CHICKEN

The salted lemons must be prepared a month in advance. The distinctive lemon and salt flavour makes it quite unlike any other chicken casserole.

For the salted lemons
8 ounces (225 g) salt
1 teaspoon peppercorns
1 teaspoon coriander seeds

3 lemons, each cut into 6 slices
juice of 1 lemon

MENU PLANNING: Serve with boiled rice and ratatouille.
Drink a Moroccan red wine.

1. Mix the salt, peppercorns and coriander seeds together and rub into the lemon slices.
2. Pack tightly into a glass jar.
3. Pour on the lemon juice then cover the jar and keep in a cool place for at least a month. As slices are removed, more fresh slices can be added to the brine, pushing them well down into the jar, but use the slices in the order in which they have been salted. Top up the jar with lemon juice if necessary.

For the Moroccan chicken
3 tablespoons olive oil
6 large chicken joints
8 ounces (225 g) onions, chopped
8 ounces (225 g) red peppers, chopped
1 clove of garlic, crushed
½ teaspoon ground ginger
¼ teaspoon ground cinnamon

6 slices salted lemon, rinsed
1½ lb (750 g) small new potatoes, scraped
1 ounce (25 g) flaked almonds
1 ounce (25 g) stoned black olives

Salting 1 month
Preparation 10 minutes
Cooking 1 hour

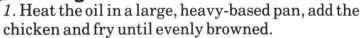

1. Heat the oil in a large, heavy-based pan, add the chicken and fry until evenly browned.
2. Add the onions, peppers, garlic, ginger, cinnamon and 6 lemon slices. Cover and cook for 10 minutes.
3. Add 1 pint (600 ml) water, cover and simmer until the chicken is nearly tender – about 15 minutes.
4. Add the potatoes, almonds and olives, cover and simmer for another 15 minutes.

CONQUEROR'S GAME BIRD

We invented this dish in honour of the 900th anniversary of *Domesday Book,* using ingredients which William I's cooks would have had to hand.

3½-4 lb (1.5-1.75 kg)
  chicken
2 parsnips, chopped
1 onion, chopped
2 cloves of garlic, chopped
3 bay leaves
sprigs of fresh thyme,
  marjoram and basil
6 juniper berries, crushed
2 teaspoons salt

2 tablespoons vinegar
1 pint (600 ml) red wine
2 ounces (50 g) butter
2 tablespoons flour

Marinating 4 days
Preparation 10 minutes
Cooking 2 hours 35
  minutes
Temperature 275°F
  (140°C) gas mark 1

MENU PLANNING: Serve with bread sauce, game chips and Brussels sprouts. Drink a good claret, or Cabernet from California or Bulgaria.

1. Put the chicken into a bowl that it just fits, pack the vegetables, herbs and spices around, sprinkle on the salt and vinegar and pour on sufficient wine to more than half cover it.

2. Keep in the refrigerator and turn daily for 4 days.

3. Remove the chicken and pat it dry. Strain the marinade and reserve.

4. Heat the butter in a large frying pan and brown the chicken evenly. Remove the chicken.

5. Stir the flour into the frying pan then gradually add 1 pint (600 ml) of the strained marinade and heat until it thickens to a thin sauce.

6. Put the chicken in an oven-proof casserole, pour the sauce over, cover and cook for 2 hours at 275°F (140°C) gas mark 1, or at the lowest temperature at which your oven functions efficiently.

7. Remove the chicken and keep warm on a serving dish.

8. Boil the liquid until reduced to a thickish sauce. Pour half over the chicken and serve the rest separately.

CHICKEN WITH 40 BAY LEAVES

A dish for anyone with a flourishing bay tree who can never think of enough uses for the leaves. They should be hung in a warm room for 2 or 3 weeks before they are used.

2 tablespoons olive oil
2 ounces (50 g) butter
40 bay leaves
5 cloves of garlic, crushed
2 ounces (50 g) flour
salt and black pepper
3½-4 lb (1.5-1.75 kg)
  roasting chicken, jointed
  (see page 13)
¼ pint (150 ml) thick cream

juice of 1 lemon
2 tablespoons brandy or
  grappa

Preparation 10 minutes
Cooking 1 hour 45 minutes
Temperature 300°F
  (150°C) gas mark 2

MENU PLANNING: Serve with a potato and celeriac purée and baked onions. Drink a dry red wine, say Chianti.

1. Heat the oil and butter in a large frying pan then add the bay leaves and garlic and fry until crisp. Don't be timid.
2. Season the flour with salt and pepper and use to coat the chicken.
3. Push the bay leaves and garlic to one side and fry the chicken in the same pan until evenly browned.
4. Transfer the chicken, bay leaves and juices to an oven-proof casserole, cover and cook for 1¼ hours at 300°F (150°C) gas mark 2.*
5. Remove the chicken and keep warm.
6. Stir the cream and lemon juice into the casserole and reheat. Do not boil or remove the bay leaves.
7. Pour over the chicken.
8. Heat the brandy or grappa in a ladle or tablespoon over a naked flame until it ignites and pour over the chicken before serving.

ARGENTINA

This Argentinian recipe, which includes the liver and heart of the chicken, depends for its characteristic flavour on cumin and cinnamon.

3½-4 lb (1.5-1.75 kg) roasting chicken
1 tablespoon vinegar
1 tablespoon lemon juice
1 clove of garlic, crushed
2 ounces (50 g) butter
8 ounces (225 g) green peppers, chopped
8 ounces (225 g) onions, chopped
1 teaspoon ground cumin
1 teaspoon ground cinnamon
3-4 teaspoons chopped fresh herbs – sage, thyme, marjoram and chives

salt and black pepper
4 ounces (100 g) ham, chopped
chicken's liver and heart, chopped
4 eggs, beaten
1 ounce (25 g) fresh breadcrumbs

Marinating 3 hours
Preparation 25 minutes
Cooking 1 hour 30 minutes
Temperature 375°F (190°C) gas mark 5 for 20 minutes

MENU PLANNING: Serve with pommes Anna and broad beans or courgettes. Drink a Spanish red wine.

1. Marinate the chicken for 3 hours in 1½ pints (900 ml) water, the vinegar, lemon juice and garlic.
2. Transfer the chicken to a saucepan, almost cover with the marinade, bring to the boil, cover and simmer gently for 45 minutes.
3. Remove the chicken, allow it to cool slightly then remove the skin and take the flesh from the bones.
4. Heat 1 ounce (25 g) butter in a frying pan, add the peppers and onions and fry until soft.
5. Stir in the cumin, cinnamon, herbs, salt, pepper, ham and the chicken's liver and heart.
6. Stir in the eggs and heat until they start to set.
7. Put a layer of this mixture in an oven-proof casserole, then add a layer of chicken meat, and continue to alternate the layers until both are used up, ending with the egg mixture.
8. Top with the breadcrumbs and dabs of the remaining butter.
9. Bake for 20 minutes at 375°F (190°C) gas mark 5.

LE VRAI COQ AU VIN*

Undistinguished attempts at Coq au vin must outnumber all other culinary disappointments. This magnificent and apparently simple dish is hard to cook well. The main problem is a sauce that is too thin. The solution is *not* to use less wine, *nor* to thicken it with more flour, but to reduce the wine by boiling before you start. This is more important than using a fine wine. Any robust red wine will do.

1 bottle robust red wine
4 bay leaves
2 sprigs of fresh thyme or
  1 teaspoon of dried thyme
2 cloves of garlic, crushed
1 carrot, chopped
4 ounces (100 g) smoked
  bacon, diced
12-16 small onions
3-4 lb (1.5-1.75 kg)
  roasting chicken, jointed
  (see page 13)
approximately 1½ ounces

(40 g) butter
2 tablespoons brandy
4 ounces (100 g)
  mushrooms, stalks
  removed
½ tablespoon flour
salt and pepper
For serving
6 small slices of fried bread

Preparation 10 minutes
Cooking 1 hour 30 minutes

MENU PLANNING: Serve with plain boiled potatoes and French beans.
Drink the same type of wine that has been used in the recipe.

1. Boil the wine with 2 bay leaves, 1 sprig of thyme, 1 clove of garlic and the carrot until reduced by half. Strain and reserve.
2. Cook the bacon and the onions in a large, heavy-based saucepan, stirring occasionally, until the onions start to colour.
3. Remove the onions and bacon with a slotted spoon, add the chicken and fry until evenly browned, adding a little butter if necessary to prevent it sticking.
4. Heat the brandy, a tablespoon at a time, over a naked flame until it ignites, then pour over the chicken.
5. Replace the onions and bacon. Pour in the reduced wine, add a sprig of thyme, the remaining garlic and bay leaves, and simmer, covered, for 20 minutes.
6. Turn the chicken joints and cook for 15 minutes.
7. Add the mushrooms and cook for 5 minutes.

8. Transfer the chicken, mushrooms, onions and bacon to a warmed dish and keep warm.

9. Blend ½ ounce (15 g) butter with ½ tablespoon flour. Stir in a little sauce then pour back into the saucepan and bring to the boil, stirring, then simmer for 2 minutes.

10. Taste for seasoning, pour over the chicken and serve with small slices of fried bread.

AVOCADO RAGOÛT

A rich and spicy French method of combining chicken with avocado.

3½ lb (1.5 kg) roasting
  chicken, jointed (see page
  13)
salt and black pepper
2 ounces (50 g) butter
1 large or 2 small onions,
  chopped
½ teaspoon medium-
  strength curry powder

½ pint (300 ml) chicken
  stock (see page 22)
2 ripe avocados
pinch of cayenne pepper
2 tablespoons thick cream

Preparation 15 minutes
Cooking 1 hour

MENU PLANNING: Serve with fried potatoes and a lettuce and chicory salad. Drink a white Burgundy or Rioja.

1. Season the chicken joints with salt and pepper.
2. Heat 1 ounce (25 g) butter in a large frying pan and fry the onions over a moderate heat until lightly coloured. Add the chicken joints and cook until evenly browned – stir occasionally to prevent the onions burning.
3. Sprinkle the curry powder into the pan, add the stock, cover and simmer over a medium heat for 30 minutes. Remove the chicken and keep warm. Reserve the juices.
4. Meanwhile, cut the firmer parts of the avocados into cubes about ½ inch (1.25 cm) square. Reserve the rest.
5. Heat the remaining butter in a small saucepan, add the avocado cubes and season with salt, pepper and a pinch of cayenne pepper. Stir gently, cover and cook over a low heat for 5 minutes, shaking the pan occasionally to prevent the avocado sticking.
6. Blend the remaining avocado flesh with the cream then stir in the chicken juices and whisk for 2-3 minutes. Pour over the avocado cubes and heat gently for a couple of minutes.
7. Place the chicken on a serving dish and pour the avocado mixture over.

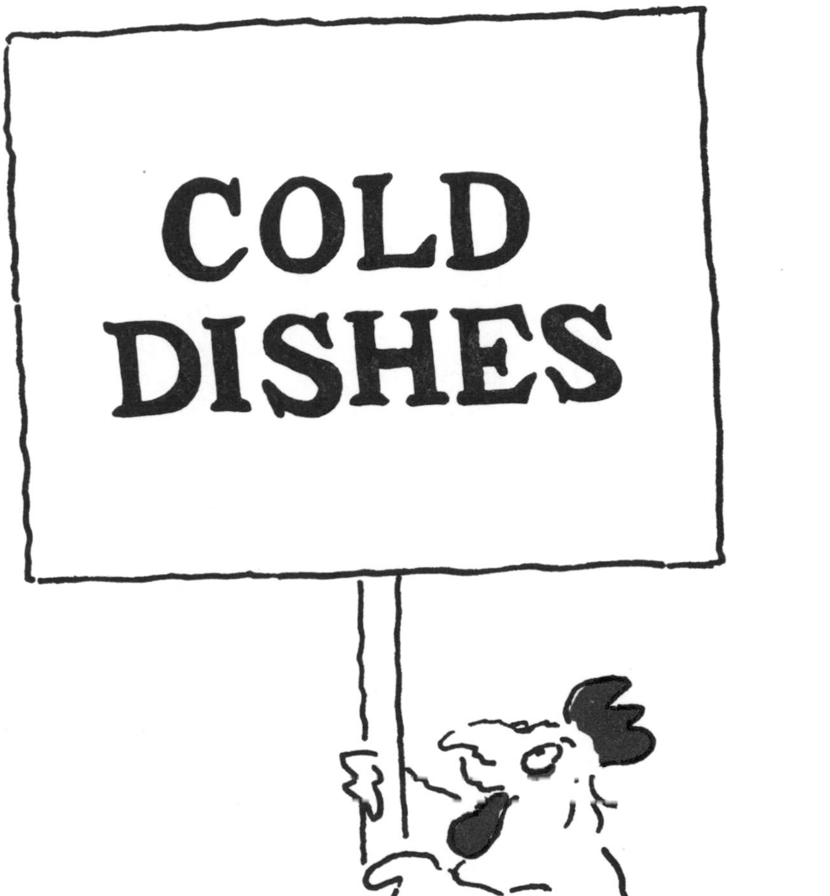
COLD
DISHES

DORSET PIE

This pie is good hot but even better cold when the juice turns to a delicious jelly.

2½-3 lb (1.25-1.5 kg)
 roasting chicken, jointed
 (see page 13)
4-5 sticks of celery,
 chopped
2 onions, chopped
12 black peppercorns
3 or 4 sprigs of fresh thyme
 or 1 teaspoon dried thyme
½ teaspoon grated nutmeg
salt
For the pastry
5 ounces (150 g) plain flour
salt
2½ ounces (65 g)
 margarine

8 ounces (225 g)
 mushrooms, chopped
¾ ounce (20 g) butter
1 bacon knuckle, smoked if
 possible, or 1 lb (450 g)
 bacon
4 or 5 sprigs fresh parsley,
 chopped

Preparation 30 minutes
Cooking 1 hour 45 minutes
Cooling 45 minutes
 (stock), 3 hours (pie)
Temperature 350°F
 (180°C) gas mark 4

MENU PLANNING: Serve
with coleslaw salad.
Drink cider.

1. Put the chicken, celery, onions, peppercorns, thyme, nutmeg and salt into a saucepan, cover with cold water, cover the pan and bring to the boil then simmer until tender – about 45 minutes.
2. For the pastry, sieve the flour and salt into a bowl, add the margarine and rub into the flour until the mixture resembles breadcrumbs. Bind to a dough with approximately 2 tablespoons water. Cover and chill for 30 minutes.
3. Remove the chicken from the pan and allow to cool slightly before removing the skin and taking the meat off the bone.
4. Strain the stock and leave to cool completely then remove all the fat from the surface.
5. Meanwhile, heat the butter in a frying pan and cook the mushrooms over a moderate heat to extract their liquid and then drain them thoroughly.
6. Remove the meat from the bacon knuckle and slice it thinly.

7. Layer the chicken, bacon and mushrooms in a 1½ pint (900 ml) pie dish sprinkling parsley and salt and pepper between the layers. Pour in sufficient stock to just cover.

8. Roll the pastry out on a lightly floured surface to the same shape as the pie dish, but slightly larger. Cut a strip from around the edge of the pastry and place on the rim of the dish. Dampen the pastry rim. Place the remaining pastry centrally on the dish and press the edge of the pastry lightly on to the lining strip. Make a small slit in the centre with the point of a sharp knife. Bake for 35 minutes at 350°F (180°C) gas mark 4.

9. Cool for 3 hours.

TUNISIAN SALAD

A simple salad for which you can use left-over rice, but it is more interesting if you prepare the special flavoured rice that we describe.

1 teaspoon oil
12 ounces (350 g) long-grain rice
1 onion, finely chopped
1 ounce (25 g) sultanas
1 ounce (25 g) flaked almonds
¼ teaspoon ground cinnamon
3 ripe tomatoes each cut into 8 pieces

12 ounces (350 g) cold cooked chicken, chopped
2-3 tablespoons oil and vinegar dressing
1 lettuce

Preparation 15 minutes
Cooking 20 minutes
Cooling 2 hours

MENU PLANNING: Serve with cheese, chutneys and pickles.
Drink Vinho Verde.

1. Heat the oil in a heavy-based saucepan, add the rice and onion and cook until the rice is translucent.

2. Stir in the sultanas, almonds, cinnamon and 1½ times the rice's volume of water. Bring to the boil, cover and simmer until the water is absorbed – 12-14 minutes.

3. Leave to cool, uncovered.

4. Mix the tomatoes, chicken and dressing into the rice.

5. Serve surrounded by lettuce leaves.

MIRACLE CHICKEN

The important points to watch in this very simple way of cooking chicken are that you have a pan that will hold the chicken plus its skewers (these conduct the heat), that the water covers the chicken and that the lid is not lifted until the chicken is cold. The result effectively turns a young roaster into a moist and succulent boiler. If using a frozen bird make sure it is thoroughly, and freshly, thawed. Always check that the meat is cooked: the juices must be clear when the flesh is pierced with a skewer. You can serve it simply with a sprinkling of soy sauce or with the Provençal sauce given below.

*3½-4 lb (1.5-1.75 kg)
    roasting chicken*
4 tablespoons wine vinegar
4 slices of fresh root ginger
8 spring onions, chopped
salt
For the sauce
*1 medium onion, finely
    chopped*
*½ teaspoon chopped fresh
    parsley or a small pinch
    of dried parsley*
*2 anchovy fillets, finely
    chopped*

*1½ ounces (40 g) capers,
    finely chopped*
*2 hard-boiled egg yolks,
    chopped*
1 egg yolk
*8 fluid ounces (225 ml)
    olive oil*
juice of 1 lemon

Preparation 10 minutes
Cooking 10 minutes
Cooling 4 hours
Sauce 20 minutes

MENU PLANNING: Serve with a potato salad. Drink a white *vin ordinaire*.

1. Pass 4 metal skewers through the chicken from side to side.
2. Rub some of the vinegar over the chicken and pour the rest into a large pan with the ginger, spring onions, a little salt and sufficient water to cover the chicken.
3. Bring to the boil, add the chicken, bring back to the boil and simmer for 30 seconds only.
4. Turn off the heat and leave until completely cold. The chicken will then be cooked.
5. For the sauce, mix the onion, parsley, anchovy fillets and capers with the hard-boiled egg yolks then stir in the raw egg yolk.

6. Stir in the olive oil and lemon juice a few drops at a time.
7. Remove the chicken from the pan and carve it into neat slices. Serve accompanied by the sauce.

COUNTRY SALAD

This simple salad depends for its excellence on fresh crisp lettuce and home-made mayonnaise.

For the mayonnaise
2 small egg yolks
½ teaspoon mustard
  powder
salt
pinch of cayenne pepper
2½ fluid ounces (65 ml)
  olive oil
1 tablespoon white wine
  vinegar
For the salad
12 ounces (350 g) cooked
  chicken, diced
approximately 14 ounce
  (400 g) can bean shoots

2 sticks of celery, diced
1 tablespoon French
  dressing
1 teaspoon soy sauce
For serving
1 large crisp lettuce
4 ounces (100 g) green
  olives, stoned

Preparation 20-25
  minutes
Cooking none

MENU PLANNING: Serve
with rye bread and spring
onions.
Drink white wine.

1. For the mayonnaise, blend the egg yolks with the mustard, salt and cayenne pepper then very gradually beat in the oil to give a thick sauce. Beat in the vinegar.
2. Mix the chicken, bean shoots and celery together, then toss in the French dressing and sprinkle on the soy sauce.
3. Mix the chicken mixture with the mayonnaise and serve on a plate of lettuce, topped with green olives.

HOENDER PASTEI

All too often the contents of a chicken pie are awash with thin and uninteresting juice. In this excellent and unusual recipe from South Africa the chicken is cooked separately so the juices can be reduced and added at the last minute. Removing the chicken flesh from the bones is our own suggestion, but not essential.

3½-4 lb (1.5-1.75 kg) roasting chicken, skinned and jointed (see page 13)
chicken's skin
2 blades of mace
1 teaspoon allspice
salt and black pepper
1 pint (600 ml) chicken stock (see page 22)
For the pastry
6 ounces (175 g) self-raising flour
salt
2½ ounces (65 g) lard or butter, diced

1 teaspoon lime pickle
2 hard-boiled eggs, sliced
2-4 ounces (50-100 g) sliced ham
2-4 ounces (50-100 g) mushrooms, sliced if necessary
1 tablespoon flour

Preparation 45 minutes
Cooking 1 hour 30 minutes
Temperature 425°F (220°C) gas mark 7 for the last 20-25 minutes
Cooling 3 hours

MENU PLANNING: Serve with a mixed salad. Drink a dry white South African wine.

1. Simmer the chicken and skin, with the mace, allspice, salt and pepper in the stock in a covered saucepan until tender – about 30 minutes.
2. For the pastry, sieve the flour and salt into a bowl, add the lard or butter and rub the fat into the flour with the fingertips. Bind to a soft, pliable dough with about 2 tablespoons cold water. Knead lightly then cover and leave in the refrigerator for 30 minutes.
3. Remove the chicken from the stock, allow to cool a little then remove the flesh from the bones.
4. Mix the flesh with the lime pickle then arrange alternate layers of chicken, egg, ham and mushrooms in a 1½ pint (900 ml) pie dish. The dish should be well filled to support the pastry.

5. Roll out the pastry on a lightly floured surface to the same shape as the pie dish, but slightly larger. Cut a strip from around the edge of the pastry and place on the rim of the pie dish. Dampen the strip of pastry. Place the remaining pastry centrally over the pie dish. Lightly press the edge of the pastry on to the lining strip. Make a small hole in the centre of the pastry with the point of a sharp knife.

6. Bake for about 20 minutes at 425°F (220°C) gas mark 7, until the pastry is a light golden brown.

7. Meanwhile, blend the flour with a little of the stock and boil the remainder until reduced to ½ pint (300 ml).

8. Gradually stir some of the hot stock into the blended flour then pour it back into the pan and boil, stirring constantly, until thickened.

9. Pour the thickened stock into the hole in the pie crust and leave to cool for 3 hours.

CHEF'S SALAD

A rich salad with an interesting combination of tastes. An excellent way of using left-over chicken.

8-12 ounces (225-350 g) cooked chicken, chopped
4 ounces (100 g) ham, chopped
4 ounces (100 g) Gruyère or Emmental cheese, chopped
4 ounces (100 g) cashew nuts

For the mayonnaise
½ teaspoon powdered mustard
salt and pepper
1 egg yolk, beaten
¼ pint (150 ml) olive oil
2 teaspoons wine vinegar
Worcestershire sauce

Preparation 15-20 minutes
Cooking none

MENU PLANNING: Serve with a green salad and wholemeal bread.
Drink a dry fruity white wine, say an Alsatian Traminer.

1. Mix the chicken, ham, cheese and nuts together.
2. For the mayonnaise, stir the mustard, salt and pepper into the egg yolk then add the oil, a few drops at a time, stirring continuously. You can use an electric whisk or a blender or liquidiser.
3. When all the oil has been added and the mayonnaise is stiff and shiny, mix in the vinegar and a few shakes of Worcestershire sauce.
4. Stir the mayonnaise into the chicken mixture.

CURRY CREAM

This is primarily a way of using left-over cooked chicken, but it is so good that it is worth cooking a chicken especially for the purpose.

½ pint (300 ml) thick cream
2 fluid ounces (50 ml) thin cream
2-4 teaspoons curry powder, to taste
salt and black pepper
6 cooked chicken joints, skinned

Preparation 15 minutes
Cooking none

1. Stir the creams, curry powder and salt and pepper together.
2. Dip the chicken joints into the cream mixture and place on a serving dish. Pour any of the cream that is left over the chicken.

POLLO IN SALSA TONNATA

This classic Italian dish is recommended for those who find their stomachs weakened in very hot weather. It is also an ideal way of serving cold, post-Christmas turkey.

*2½-3 lb (1.25-1.5 kg)
   roasting chicken or about
   1½ lb (750 g) cooked
   chicken or turkey
6 black peppercorns
salt and black pepper
1 tablespoon olive oil*
**For the tuna fish
   mayonnaise**
*3½ ounce (90 g) can tuna
   fish in oil*

*4 anchovy fillets
¼ pint (150 ml) olive oil
1 tablespoon lemon juice or
   white wine vinegar
2 egg yolks
black pepper
1 tablespoon capers*

*Preparation 20 minutes
Cooking 45 minutes
Cooling 4 hours*

1. Poach the chicken, if using an uncooked bird, with the peppercorns in salted water until tender – 30-45 minutes.
2. Remove the chicken and allow to cool slightly, before taking off the skin and removing the meat from the bones.
3. Put the chicken meat on to a plate, sprinkle with a little salt and black pepper and pour the olive oil over. Leave to cool.
4. For the tuna fish mayonnaise, mash the tuna fish and anchovies with a little olive oil or mix in a blender or liquidiser. Mix in the lemon juice or vinegar, egg yolks and a little pepper.
5. Very, very gradually stir in the rest of the oil.
6. Stir in the capers and pour the mayonnaise over the chicken.

CHICKEN IN ASPIC

This simple and reliable recipe makes an excellent picnic or party dish. But be careful, it is rich and you can easily eat too much.

3½ lb (1.5 kg) roasting
  chicken
salt
10 black peppercorns
sherry or brandy, to taste
  (optional)
½ ounce (15 g) aspic
  powder

1 egg yolk
¼ pint (150 ml) thick cream
cayenne pepper, to taste

Preparation none
Cooking 2 hours
Cooling 4 hours

MENU PLANNING: Serve with fresh raw vegetables – grated carrot, celery sticks, lettuce, cucumber or tomatoes.

1. Put the chicken, salt and peppercorns into a saucepan and cover with cold water. Bring to the boil, cover, and simmer until tender – about 35-45 minutes.
2. Remove the chicken from the water and leave to cool slightly then discard the skin, take the meat from the bones and mince it.
3. To make the aspic, add 1 pint (600 ml) boiling water (and a little sherry or brandy if you like) to the aspic powder then leave in a bowl to cool slightly.
4. Separately mix the chicken with the egg yolk and 3 teaspoons of the warm aspic. Leave to cool completely.
5. Fold in the cream, and add salt and cayenne pepper to taste.
6. When the aspic in the bowl has formed into jelly about 1 inch (2.5 cm) thick round the sides, ladle out the liquid centre, put in the chicken mixture, then pour the liquid back.
7. Leave in the refrigerator to set.
8. Turn out by dipping the bowl in hot water for a few seconds then inverting it on to a plate.

CRÊPES TERESA

An excellent dish to make from a small amount of cooked chicken. Any sort of cheese can be used, but a hard, strong cheese like Parmesan is best.

For the cheese sauce
2 ounces (50 g) butter
2 ounces (50 g) flour
1¼ pints (750 ml) milk
1½ ounces (40 g) cheese, grated
black pepper
For the filling
8 ounces (225 g) cooked chicken, minced
8 ounces (225 g) cooked spinach
1½ ounces (40 g) cheese, grated

salt
For the pancakes
4 ounces (100 g) plain flour
salt
1 egg, beaten
½ pint (300 ml) milk
approximately 2 tablespoons oil

Preparation 10 minutes
Cooking 15 minutes

MENU PLANNING: Serve with baked onions. Drink a fruity red wine, say Beaujolais.

1. For the cheese sauce, melt the butter in a small saucepan, then stir in the flour and cook for 1 minute. Gradually stir in the milk then bring to the boil, stirring. Simmer for 2 minutes then remove from the heat and stir in the cheese and pepper.
2. For the filling, mix all the ingredients together with ½ pint (300 ml) of the sauce to make a stiff paste.
3. For the pancakes, sieve the flour and salt into a bowl and make a well in the centre. Drop the egg into the well then gradually pour in the milk, stirring constantly to draw the flour into the liquid.
4. Heat a little oil in a non-stick frying pan, add 1-2 tablespoons of the batter, tilt the pan so the batter covers the surface and cook for about 3 minutes until golden and set on the underside. Turn the pancake over and cook the other side until browned. Remove and fill with the chicken mixture. Roll the pancake up and place in a shallow oven-proof dish. Make 5 more pancake rolls in a similar way, adding more oil to the frying pan as it is needed.
5. Cover the pancake rolls with the remaining sauce and place under a hot grill to brown.

RISOTTO ALLA MILANESE

Use either cooked chicken or cooked chicken liver —
both are suitable. Cooked peas are a nice addition.
Beef marrow is not easy to buy and you will probably
have to extract your own or substitute a beef cube.

2 ounces (50 g) butter
1 small onion, finely
  chopped
1 ounce (25 g) beef marrow
12 ounces (350 g) short-
  grain rice
3 fluid ounces (75 ml) dry
  white wine
1 pint (600 ml) chicken
  stock (see page 22)
6-8 saffron strands,
  crushed and steeped in a
  little hot stock for 5
  minutes

1 ounce (25 g) grated
  Parmesan cheese
6-8 ounces (175-225 g)
  cooked chicken or chicken
  livers, chopped
salt and black pepper

Preparation 10 minutes
Cooking 40 minutes

MENU PLANNING: No
vegetables needed.
Drink a red or white Italian
wine.

1. Heat 1 ounce (25 g) butter in a large frying pan, add
the onion and cook gently until softened.
2. Stir in the marrow and the rice and cook, stirring,
until the grains become translucent.
3. Stir in the wine and increase the heat. Boil the
mixture until nearly all the liquid has evaporated.
4. Stir in the stock, stir once, cover and simmer for 14
minutes until the liquid has been absorbed and the
rice is tender.
5. Stir in the saffron and soaking liquor, cheese and
remaining butter, then place the chicken or chicken
liver on top for a couple of minutes to heat through.
6. Stir all the ingredients together and taste for
seasoning.

SIMPLE SWEET AND SOUR

This way of incorporating chicken in a pineapple sweet-sour sauce is a great deal simpler than the result suggests. The sauce can be prepared ahead.

For the sauce
1 tablespoon oil
2 tablespoons wine vinegar
2-3 teaspoons sugar
salt
15 ounce (425 g) can
  crushed pineapple,
  drained
2 tablespoons cornflour

For the chicken
8-12 ounces (225-350 g)
  cooked chicken, chopped
1 egg, beaten
2 tablespoons cornflour
2 tablespoons oil

Preparation 5 minutes
Cooking 25 minutes

MENU PLANNING: Serve with boiled rice and broccoli or cauliflower. Drink green tea.

1. For the sauce bring the oil, vinegar, sugar, salt and 2 tablespoons water to the boil.
2. Add the pineapple.
3. Blend the cornflour with 2 tablespoons water, stir into the pineapple mixture and heat gently, stirring until it thickens.
4. Mix the chicken and egg together.
5. Sprinkle on the cornflour and stir all together.
6. Heat the oil in a frying pan, add the chicken and fry briskly for 2-3 minutes, until it begins to become crisp.
7. Drain the chicken on absorbent paper then stir into the sauce and cook gently for 2 minutes. If the sauce seems too thick, add some of the pineapple juice.

CHICKEN CUTLETS

This economical dish makes use of cooked rice as well as cooked chicken.

1 ounce (25 g) butter
1 ounce (25 g) flour
¼ pint (150 ml) chicken
  stock (see page 22)
8 ounces (225 g) cooked
  chicken, minced
2 ounces (50 g) boiled long-
  grain rice

2 heaped teaspoons capers
salt and black pepper
2 ounces (50 g) dried
  breadcrumbs
4 tablespoons oil

Preparation 5 minutes
Chilling 1 hour
Cooking 25 minutes

1. Melt the butter in a heavy-based saucepan, stir in the flour then gradually stir in the stock and bring to the boil, stirring. Simmer for 2 minutes.
2. Stir the chicken, rice, capers, salt and pepper into the sauce. Leave to cool.
3. Spoon large tablespoonfuls, one at a time, on to the breadcrumbs and turn them until evenly coated. Shape into cutlets and chill until firm.
4. Heat the oil in a frying pan, and fry the cutlets briskly on each side until evenly crisp and browned then more gently for no more than 15 minutes in total.
5. Drain on absorbent paper.

CHICKEN IN BAKED APPLES

This Arabic dish is too exotic for some friends who claim not to know whether they are eating a main course or a sweet, but we find it delicious. It is important to hollow out the apples as we describe.

6 large cooking apples, cored
3 ounces (75 g) butter
1 ounce (25 g) cooked rice
6 ounces (175 g) cooked chicken, diced
1 ounce (25 g) sultanas
½ teaspoon ground cinnamon

1 hard-boiled egg, diced
3 teaspoons clear honey

Preparation 25 minutes
Cooking 30 minutes
Temperature 350°F (180°C) gas mark 4

1. Enlarge the hollows in the apples to at least the size of a golf ball with a sharp-edged teaspoon.
2. Melt 2 ounces (50 g) butter in a baking tin and add the apples.
3. Melt the remaining butter.
4. Divide the rice then the melted butter between the hollows in the apples.
5. Mix the chicken, sultanas, cinnamon and hard-boiled egg together and spoon into the apples.
6. Top each apple with ½ teaspoon honey.
7. Bake for 30 minutes at 350°F (180°C) gas mark 4, basting with the butter every 10 minutes.

OHIO CHICKEN

A delicious farmhouse recipe for cooked chicken, but a little more tricky than it sounds. The secrets are to add sufficient stock and to use plenty of oil for frying. If, nevertheless, the 'cake' breaks apart, just stir all the ingredients together and serve. It will still taste good.

12 ounces (350 g) cooked chicken, finely diced
12 ounces (350 g) boiled potatoes, finely diced
6-8 tablespoons chicken stock (see page 22)

salt and black pepper
4 tablespoons oil
3 onions, sliced

Preparation 10 minutes
Cooking 25 minutes

MENU PLANNING: Serve with sweetcorn and a green salad.
Drink lager.

1. Mix the chicken, potatoes, stock, salt and pepper together to form a thick, creamy mixture.
2. Heat the oil in a large frying pan, add the onions and fry until they begin to colour.
3. Add the chicken mixture, pat it down flat and fry briskly until the bottom is crisp.
4. Fold the 'cake' over like an omelette and serve.

CHICKEN RICE

This modestly titled recipe makes a similar but more homey risotto than the one on page 117.

1 onion, chopped
12 ounces (350 g) rice
21 fluid ounces (625 ml) chicken stock (see page 22)
1 ounce (25 g) cheese, grated
2 ounces (50 g) sultanas, optional

salt and black pepper
6-8 ounces (175-225 g) cooked chicken, chopped
1 ounce (25 g) butter

Preparation 50 minutes
Cooking 45 minutes
Temperature 350°F (180°) gas mark 4

MENU PLANNING: No vegetables needed.
Drink a red or white *vin ordinaire.*

1. Stir all the ingredients together in an oven-proof casserole.
2. Cover and cook for 45 minutes at 350°F (180°C) gas mark 4.

JUTLAND BLUE

Our cousin, Sebastian, who is a quarter Danish, brought back this delicious method of using up cooked chicken. In Jutland they of course use the local Jutland cheese, but any Danish blue cheese can be substituted.

½ ounce (15 g) butter
4-6 ounces (100-175 g)
  mushrooms, chopped
2 cloves of garlic, crushed
10 ounces (300 g) cooked
  chicken, minced
1 egg
1 teaspoon caraway seeds
salt and black pepper
6 large thin slices of cooked
  ham

For the sauce
1½ ounces (40 g) butter
2 ounces (50 g) flour
1 pint (600 ml) milk
6 ounces (175 g) Jutland or
  other Danish blue cheese,
  grated or finely crumbled
black pepper

Preparation 10 minutes
Cooking 40 minutes
Temperature 350°F
  (180°C) gas mark 4

MENU PLANNING: Precede
with Danish herrings and
neat aquavit.
Drink lager.

1. Heat the butter in a frying pan, add the mushrooms and garlic and fry until just soft, stirring occasionally.
2. Stir in the chicken, egg, caraway seeds, salt and pepper.
3. Divide the chicken between the slices of ham. Roll the slices up and place side by side in a flat, shallow baking dish.
4. For the sauce, melt the butter in a saucepan, stir in the flour and cook, stirring, for 1 minute then gradually stir in the milk. Bring to the boil, still stirring, then simmer for 2 minutes. Remove from the heat and stir in 4½ ounces (115 g) cheese and the pepper.
5. Pour the sauce over the ham rolls and top with the remaining cheese.
6. Bake for 20 minutes at 350°F (180°C) gas mark 4 then brown under a hot grill.

STUFFED AUBERGINES

We describe the basic method, and give a mixture of ingredients which makes a good filling, but these can be almost infinitely varied.

3 aubergines about ½ lb
  (225 g) each
2 ounces (50 g) butter
1 onion, chopped
2 ounces (50 g)
  mushrooms, chopped
2 tomatoes, skinned and
  chopped
1 clove of garlic, crushed
6-8 ounces (175-225 g)
  cooked chicken, minced
2 ounces (50 g) cooked rice
1 tablespoon tomato purée

2 ounces (50 g) cheese,
  grated
salt and black pepper
2 ounces (50 g) fresh
  breadcrumbs

Preparation 10 minutes
Cooking 1 hour
Temperature 350°F
  (180°C) gas mark 4

MENU PLANNING: Serve with fried potatoes and sautéed red peppers. Drink a red Greek wine.

1. Cut the aubergines in half lengthways and simmer, cut-side down, in a little water in a large covered pan for about 20 minutes.
2. Meanwhile, melt 1 ounce (25 g) butter, add the onion, mushrooms and tomatoes and cook gently until soft, stirring occasionally.
3. Remove the aubergines from the water, and allow them to drain well. Place the aubergines cut-side uppermost in a baking dish and scoop out the centres with a teaspoon but using a knife to cut through the fibres at the stalk end. Take care not to break the skin.
4. Chop the aubergine flesh and mix it with the onion, mushrooms and tomatoes then stir in the garlic, chicken, rice, tomato purée, grated cheese, salt and pepper. If the mixture seems dry, moisten it with a little stock or water.
5. Spoon the mixture into the aubergine skins then dot with the remaining butter and sprinkle the breadcrumbs evenly over the tops.
6. Bake for 20 minutes at 350°F (180°C) gas mark 4 then place under a hot grill for a few minutes to brown.

WHITE NEWBURG

This is similar to the better-known Lobster Newburg. It should be made with chicken that has been cooked by a simple method, otherwise the delicate flavour of the Newburg will be spoilt.

3 ounces (75 g) rendered
  chicken fat or butter
4 ounces (100 g)
  mushrooms, sliced
1¼ lb (500 g) cooked
  chicken, chopped
4 fluid ounces (100 ml) dry
  sherry
¼ pint (150 ml) thin cream

3 egg yolks
salt and black pepper
For serving
6 slices of toast
paprika

Preparation 10 minutes
Cooking 30 minutes

MENU PLANNING: Drink a light white wine.

1. Heat the chicken fat or butter in a frying pan, add the mushrooms and cook lightly until just softened.
2. Add the chicken and half the sherry and cook for 2-3 minutes.
3. Transfer the mixture to a double saucepan or a bowl over a saucepan of simmering water, stir in the cream and heat, stirring occasionally, for 2-3 minutes.
4. Blend the egg yolks with a little of the warm juice, then stir them into the chicken mixture with the remaining sherry.
5. Continue to heat, stirring, until the sauce thickens.
6. Add salt and pepper to taste. Serve on hot toast sprinkled with paprika.

CANNELLONI

Though we don't pretend that our chicken cannelloni is the genuine thing it is nevertheless extremely good, and a convenient way of using up a small quantity of cold chicken.

1 ounce (25 g) butter
1 onion, finely chopped
3 ounces (75 g) chicken livers
6 ounces (175 g) cooked chicken, minced
1 egg
2 ounces (50 g) grated Parmesan cheese
salt and black pepper

12 cannelloni squares (home made) or ready-made cases
¼ pint (150 ml) chicken stock (see page 22)

Preparation 15 minutes
Cooking 35 minutes
Temperature 350°F (180°C) gas mark 4

MENU PLANNING: Serve with a mixed salad. Drink Chianti.

1. Heat half the butter in a frying pan, add the onion and fry until softened.
2. Add the chicken livers and fry for 2 minutes.
3. Mince the onions and liver together then mix with the chicken, egg, half the cheese, salt and pepper.
4. Wrap this mixture in the cannelloni squares, or fill the cases. Do not pack them too tightly or they will be heavy.
5. Grease an oven-proof dish that the cannelloni will almost fill with the remaining butter. Lay the stuffed cannelloni side by side in the dish.
6. Bring the stock almost to boiling point and pour over the cannelloni.
7. Sprinkle with the remaining cheese.
8. Cover and cook for 15 minutes at 350°F (180°C) gas mark 4.
9. Uncover and brown lightly under a hot grill.

GALANTINE PARFAIT

Not only does this taste extremely good but it looks magnificent when served and carved. Practise first before serving it at a dinner party as it may take you well over half an hour to bone the bird and your initial attempt may not look all it should. It is also delicious cold.

3½ lb (1.5 kg) roasting chicken, boned (see page 14, Method A)

For the stuffing

8 ounces (225 g) chicken livers, roughly chopped

4 ounces (100 g) mushrooms, roughly chopped

6 fluid ounces (175 ml) thick cream

4 ounces (100 g) fresh breadcrumbs

1 heaped tablespoon chopped fresh parsley or 1½ tablespoons dried parsley

3 teaspoons fresh thyme or 1½ teaspoons dried thyme

1 teaspoon lemon juice

1 clove of garlic, crushed

salt and black pepper

3 ounces (75 g) butter, melted

1 egg, beaten

Preparation 1 hour 20 minutes

Cooking 1 hour 30 minutes

Temperature 375°F (190°C) gas mark 5

Cooling 4 hours

MENU PLANNING: Serve with cold spinach with an oil and vinegar dressing. Drink a red Portuguese wine, say Dão.

1. For the stuffing mix the chicken livers, mushrooms, cream, breadcrumbs, herbs, lemon juice, garlic, salt and pepper with the butter.

2. Bind together with the egg.

3. First put a little stuffing into the wings and legs then spread the remainder over the central cavity, being careful to distribute it evenly.

4. Fold the loose skin over the openings and tie the legs and wings into place, re-forming the shape of the unboned bird.

5. Place the chicken in a casserole or tin that will hold it in shape.

6. Roast for 1 hour 20 minutes at 375°F (190°C) gas mark 5.

7. Leave the chicken in the casserole or tin for 10 minutes before transferring to a warmed carving dish. Cut in thick slices to serve.

INDEX

rijstafel, 85
risotto, *see* rice
rissoles: curried fritos, 40-1
   Polish, 91
roasting, 9, 16

saffron, paella, 89
   Persian pilaf, 66-7
   risotto alla Milanese, 117
salads: chef's salad, 112
   country salad, 109
   Tunisian, 107
salting in brine, 19-20
sauté à la paysanne, 59
Senegal chicken, 96
shellfish, paella, 89
simple sweet and sour, 118
sopa picadillo, 30
soups, 21-32
Southern fried chicken, 55
soy sauce: mizutaki, 63
   white cloud, 84
spinach, crêpes Teresa, 116
spit-roasting, 16

stewing fowl, 10
stock, 22
stuffing, 13
sweet and sour, 118
sweetcorn: corn chowder, 26
   Mexican chowder, 86

terrines, *see* pâtés
thawing chickens, 12-13
thigh fillets, 15
tomato: chicken Marengo, 50
   chicken Provençal, 95
   Mexican chowder, 86
   piperade with chicken livers, 75
   stuffed aubergines, 122
tongue, grilled chicken
   Maintenon, 92
trussing chickens, 13
tuna, pollo in salsa tonnata, 113
Tunisian salad, 107

Vallé d'Auge, 78

veal: gourmet Hongroise, 87
   pâté-terrine de volaille, 38-9
velouté de volaille, 29
Le vrai coq au vin, 102-3

water chestnuts, chicken
   Chinoise, 80
watercress and chicken, 88
waterzooi, 64
West African peanut stew, 52
white cloud, 84
white Newburg, 123
wine: chicken Marengo, 50
   chicken Provençal, 95
   Conqueror's game bird, 99
   gallina en pepitoria, 62
   grilled chicken Maintenon, 92
   sauté aux olives, 94
   Le vrai coq au vin, 102-3

yoghurt: chicken yoghurt soup, 32
   kaju murgh kari, 69